"With warmth and humor Shirlene McKinney takes us through a move to southern Oregon, with the resulting crises of spoiled cats, a smart goat, a "Perpetual Remodeling," and numerous other adventures with the animals, plants and people in her life. "When His hand is upon something, it really comes together," she writes, and you'll have the fun of seeing that happen here.

Lorena McCourtney
Author of the *Ivy Malone Mystery* series

Dear Friends and Family...

By E. Shirlene McKinney

INFINITY
PUBLISHING.COM

Copyright © 2010 by E. Shirlene McKinney

ISBN 0-7414-3647-7

Published by:

INFI∞ITY
PUBLISHING.COM

1094 New DeHaven Street, Suite 100
West Conshohocken, PA 19428-2713
Info@buybooksontheweb.com
www.buybooksontheweb.com
Toll-free (877) BUY BOOK
Local Phone (610) 941-9999
Fax (610) 941-9959

Printed in the United States of America

Published January 2010

Dedication

In memory of my precious grandmother,
Emma Columbus Cooper McKinney
for whom I am named,
Emma Shirlene McKinney.
Thank you, Gram, for showing me Christ
in the way you lived your life.

In memory of my father,
Lester Osmer (Ozzie) McKinney
Wonderful father, good friend and hunting buddy.

I miss both of them more than I can say.

And to all the friends and family, who have "hung in there"
with me, throughout the years.
I love you.

Acknowledgments

No book comes to completion without the aid and support of many people. This is especially true of this book, which would have never been put into book form, had it not been for the encouragement of those to whom I have written, over the years. I would like to share some of the comments that have been written to me, from various friends and family, and thank each one for their encouragement and support.

"Thanks for the wonderful letters! Everything stops in our house when we receive them."

Elsie Danser   Reedsville, West Virginia

"My mother and I enjoy your letters, very much. As a matter of fact, she's keeping all your letters. She thinks they'll make a book, one day."

Joyce Steinmiller   Citrus Heights, CA

"Your letters read like a book—they are great. Reminds me of the book, *The Egg and I.*"

Charleene Stockdale   Sacramento CA

"I do hope you are compiling a book—it would be a best seller!"

Mary Gehr   Crescent City, CA

"Reading your *Dear Friends and Family* letters is time well spent. It reminds me of one of my favorite books, *The Egg and I.* Full of humor and realistic day-to-day living, with all its trials and tribulations."

Janelle Heatley   Post Falls, ID

"You write such interesting letters. That is the first piece of mail I open when they arrive. There is always something in them that makes me laugh. They brighten my day!"

Shirley Easler   Rosamond, CA

"It makes mom's (Mozelle Lynch) day when she gets a letter from you."   Penny Pemberton

"I can't tell you the wonderful timing of your letter. It gave me a ray of sunshine. After I read your letters, they get passed around to all of my family. They love them. You can never know the joy you bring to so many. You have a wonderful gift."

Penny and George Pemberton   Longview, TX

"You write the most interesting and pleasant letters of anyone we know. You make them funny and informative and they really brighten our day. You definitely would make a very good writer. God gave you a way of putting down words that make for enjoyable reading. We thoroughly enjoy reading everyone of them."

Beulah and Raymond Strahan   Reedsville, West Virginia

"I love getting your letters. You have the heart of a poet."

Carol Hankins   Mountain Home, AR

"We love your letters. I hope you're saving them. You could write your own *Chicken Soup For The Soul.*"

Ann and Bill Davis   Roseville, CA

"I keep all your letters. It's fun to read them over again."

Joyce Shultz   Rosamond, CA

"Your expressions are so endearing, unique and filled with humor, but come forth with great expression and a true love of nature and everyday living. Your letters are entertaining and interesting. In fact, much better than most novels these days."

Joyce and Ed McColgan   Sacramento, CA

"I enjoy your letters so much and have them clipped in sequence to read again. They are great keepsakes. Your descriptions of the outdoors, environment and the antics of your domestic and wild animals, are so vivid. You should write short stories."

Bill and Inga Wynn   Sacramento, CA

"You don't know how much I enjoy getting your letters. I read them to Donna and Rosie, and Rosie calls you the lady who writes the wonderful letters."

Nellie Dennison   Brownsville, OR

Thank you, dear friends and family, for your wonderful comments and for urging me to put these letters into a book. Without your prompting and support, I might never have done this. God has truly blessed me with wonderful friends and family. Thanks to Harry for believing I could do this. Thanks also to my editor, Jacquelyn Stout, for her encouragement and suggestions.

Letter from the Editor

I knew the author, Shirlene McKinney, by acquaintance before editing her book, *Dear Friends and Family.* Now that I have walked through many pages of her past, I now know a sincere, spiritual person of faith intermingled in a spontaneous, personable lady who enjoys lacing each day with humor and practical living.

The author has the unique ability to extract the extraordinary from the mundane. Metaphors and similes paint each page of experience and bring to life a by-gone ability to dwell in the enjoyment of the moment.

Shirlene has discovered the kingdom of God within her. Her enjoyment of each day and her ability to share it with readers through a stream-of-consciousness writing style is so interesting that one wants to peek over her fence to enjoy her next experience.

Curling up with this book will allow each reader to restore the fun that is missing from our often too-busy lives and might even revive the almost-lost art of letter writing.

I enjoy being a part of her friends and family.

Jacquelyn Stout

Introduction

After years of hoping and planning, my dream of moving back to Oregon was finally going to be realized. I had lived in Oregon for four years from 1979 to 1983; but due to my father's failing health and the fact that renters were demolishing my home in West Sacramento, I moved back to California. Knowing that my father didn't have many years to live, I promised I would not move away again as long as he was alive. We had seven good years of memory building before he passed away. It was time well spent.

I wasn't born in Oregon; in fact, I had lived most of my life in California with the exception of a few temporary moves to Nevada, Colorado and Oregon. However, even before I first set foot on Oregon soil, I was in love with this beautiful state. I always knew it was where I wanted to live. Now, in my early sixties, I was finally "coming home."

In February of 2000, I was repairing damages which renters had done to my home in West Sacramento, while my husband, an aviation mechanic specializing in helicopter rotors, had taken a job in Arizona.

In the process of getting my home ready to sell, I was trying to deal with the effects of Fibromyalgia (see glossary), Polymyalgia Rheumatica (see glossary), heart arrhythmia, arthritis and several other health problems. In my *spare* time, I was working on a fiction novel, and trying to keep track of my friends and family, scattered across the United States from West Virginia, Maryland, South Carolina, Texas, Idaho and throughout California. Initially, in an effort to keep in touch, I wrote to approximately sixty-five people. Gradually, by a process of elimination of those who never responded or made an effort to keep in touch with me, my list dwindled to thirty-two or thirty-three. Since it was impossible to write individual letters to that many people, and since I was telling everyone the same information, I started writing a *Dear Friends and Family* letter, with personalized, hand written comments at the end. Thus began a monthly diary, in letters.

The letters never started out to become a book. They were written as a friendly chat with a friend or family member, over a cup of tea or coffee. Over the years, numerous friends and family members encouraged me to compile the letters into a book, which has become *Dear Friends and Family*.

My cousin's wife, whom I have never met, told me she passes the letters on to her sister (whom I also have not met), and they pass the letters on to someone who takes them to work at the telephone company. One friend was taking them to a nursing home to read to the patients. Another told me, "When your letters arrive, everything stops and the whole family gathers around while we read them."

So, keep in mind that these were *informally written, personal letters*. If there is an occasional run-on sentence, that's the way I talk! (Blame me, not my editor.) So, grab your cup of coffee or tea and let's sit down and visit. I hope you enjoy the humor of every-day life, and that something in the letters will lift your spirits and bless you.

E. Shirlene McKinney

Part One

2000

February 28, 2000

D ear Friends and Family,

.Remodeling on the inside of this house (in West Sacramento) appears to be finally over, although I still have a couple of rooms to paint. I'm not looking forward to that, so I'm using every possible excuse to procrastinate, and finding a rather good array. "Can't do it today—it's damp and rainy; can't do it tomorrow—the sun is going to shine, and I need to work outside. I can't do it next week—I'll be busy accepting the Nobel Peace Prize for 'Excellence in Procrastination'." Well, you get the idea. Will try to get my 'For Sale' sign made and out front, by the end of this month. Usually, March, April, May and June are the best months for selling. I'm hoping that will be true this year.

After two-and-a-half months of being among the *elite* unemployed, Harry got a job with Papillon Helicopters at the Grand Canyon in Arizona. He left January 20 and reports that he is unpacked and settled in. Since they are out in the middle of nowhere, the company furnishes housing at a very reasonable rent, and Harry and two other mechanics share a four-bedroom unit. I probably will make a trip there sometime in May, after the snow melts. At the present time, Harry says it is pretty cold there, so I think I'll wait for the spring thaw.

The week before Harry left for Arizona, we were watching a program about the wildlife (animal type) in the Grand Canyon. There is a particular type of pine tree that is only found in the Grand Canyon, and a bird that survives on the pine nuts from that tree. The program moderator said, "The bird is called a Nutcracker." I looked at Harry and said, "That's a Nutcracker, sweet." He laughed and then groaned. Maybe he took the job at the Grand Canyon to get away from my puns!

I got a Compaq Presario 1600S lap-top computer and have managed to extend the amount of time I can work on the computer. Now, when I'm sitting at the desk computer and start to ache and hurt, I just move into my easy chair with my lap-top and go on working. If I remember to get up and walk around once in a while, I can usually work an extra hour or two. Pretty cushy! Now, if I can just figure out some way to prepare meals on this thing . . . .

Now that I can work a little bit longer, I am once again doing corrections on my book, *The Road Home,* (a fiction novel.) I'm beginning to wonder if I'll ever get it finished. Harry said if I have to print and correct this thing many more times, they will have to cut down more trees. That's probably true. It takes almost a whole ream of paper each time I have to re-print it. Hopefully, not too many more times.

As for aching, I usually do. I have good days and bad days, but when I have a bad day I just say, "Oh, well, tomorrow will be better." I can always look around and find someone worse off than me, so I am thankful for the blessings I have. God is good! Won't it be glorious, someday, when we stand before Jesus and have no more pain and problems? Praise God!

Much *busy*ness around here, but not much news, so I'll close this yak session and send my love and prayers to all. God Bless!

Shirlene and Harry

I somehow managed to lose the letters for March, April and May 2000, as I have no printed or computer copies. My house in West Sacramento went into escrow and I started packing and having garage sales. Harry accepted a job at Erickson Air Crane in Central Point, Oregon, and I began making trips to Oregon to look for property. It was a very busy, hectic time, and I may not have written very much during that period. But I know I wrote "something" because my next letter refers to the change of address and phone number. We moved to Oregon the end of May, on Memorial Day weekend, and the next record of letters I have begins June 2.

June 2, 2000

D ear Friends & Family,

I hope none of you have tried to call us since we moved because I inadvertently gave you a wrong phone number. Our (correct) number and address, are enclosed. We rented a house on Rogue River Highway, and the back yard ends in the River. We are at the front of the property and there is a small cottage in back, but only one mail box for both. The renter in the cottage shares our mailbox, so just put an "A" after our house number.

We left Sacramento around 11:00 a.m. on Sunday and got here sometime after 6:00 p.m. Harry drove one big rental truck, Derek drove the second one, I drove my loaded pickup pulling a trailer, and Kelly and the grandchildren followed in their car. We made quite a caravan. We still had to leave things behind that I will have to go back and get.

Since Monday was a holiday, we could only get two people to help unload. Harry had fallen off the truck while we were loading, so he was too stiff and sore to be of any help. The two workers and I worked eleven solid hours to get the two trucks, my pickup and the trailer unloaded. I started an hour before the helpers arrived and finished an hour after they left, so I put in a thirteen-hour day lifting heavy boxes. I was so tired and in so much pain at the end of the day, I was staggering. When I finally collapsed into bed, it hurt to take a deep breath. I spent most of the next day in bed and still haven't fully recuperated. I have one more load in Sacramento, but won't go back for it until next week. Just not feeling well enough to make the trip.

I've unpacked a few boxes—mostly kitchen and office items—and set up my computer today so I could get out the corrected change of address. One of our helpers in West Sacramento packed the computer equipment, and I almost panicked when I couldn't find my computer and printer cords. They weren't in the box with the computer or printer, so I finally guessed they might have been stuffed in with the fax machine (they were), which we aren't setting up for our (hopefully) short stay here.

June 3, 2000

Harry is feeling better and now has the spa filled and heating. We both need it. Harry needed the white vinegar to rinse the spa, so, standing among a mountain of boxes he asked, "Do you know where the vinegar is?" I enthusiastically nodded yes. "Oh, good! Where?"

"Packed in a box somewhere," I told him. I try to be helpful and informative whenever possible.

Last night I told Harry to lock the back door, and he looked at the maze of boxes and laughed. "A burglar would be crazy to break in here. He'd break his neck trying to get through."

"Then be sure and lock it," I told him. "We can't afford the lawsuit!"

I don't want to unpack everything and get settled in, then have to re-pack as soon as we find our property, so I'm being very selective about what gets unpacked. That has good news and bad news. The good news is I won't have so much re-packing. The bad news is, I'm trying to live among boxes stacked everywhere, which is very messy and drives me crazy. The good news is, when it starts getting to me, I can sit on the deck and watch the river.

I've heard some rivers described as 'lazy' but that certainly wouldn't apply to the Rogue. It races by here like it is late for an appointment! Even so, it *is* soothing to sit and watch it go rushing by. I guess part of it is the whole effect of river, mountains, blue sky and a symphony of nature's sounds. Bumblebees defy aerodynamics and blunder from blossom to blossom, crickets serenade their ladies with songs to woo and win, and a cacophony of twitter-pated birds chirp, whistle and screech at their intended mates. One little fellow, I'm sure, must have been rejected by the entire female bird population, for he sits outside my window at 5:30 in the morning, making a sound that can only be described as agony. (No wonder he was rejected!)

Mornings here are cool, which I love. I put on my sweater, take my devotional book, tea, toast and fresh strawberries and sit on the deck. Most days, I have breakfast and lunch on the deck and, if I could get all the boxes off the deck, we would probably have dinner there. At the end of the small back yard, there is a two-level deck. The top deck is level with the back yard, then there are stairs going down to a lower deck, which overlooks the water. With the deck off the back of the house, that gives us three usable decks. Maybe we could rent out one or two?

The weather here is about ten degrees cooler than the Sacramento Valley, which suits me just fine. It is a very pleasant eighty six degrees. Many houses in Oregon, including this one we've rented, do not have air-conditioning, because it never really gets that uncomfortable. Even when it gets fairly hot during a summer afternoon, things cool down nicely at night. When you go to bed, you open the windows and let in the cool air. In the morning, you close windows and angle the blinds to keep out the heat, and the house stays nice and cool. At least, in theory.

I moved away from Oregon seventeen years ago. It has taken me a long time to get back, but it feels like coming home. I have always loved this beautiful state, so, with God's permission and help, this will be my home for the remainder of my life. I'm scheduled to go looking at property on Monday with my Realtor, and praying for God's guidance in finding the right piece of land. We found a manufactured home that we both like, that will work for us. I'm sure God's hand will guide us in finding property. Isn't God good?! With that thought, I bid you so-long for now. Sending our love and prayers,

Shirlene and Harry

After unpacking a few boxes and resting up a bit, I made another trip back to Sacramento to get items we had left behind in the original move—mostly plants that were in large containers. I brought back a pickup load and pulled a trailer full of plants. Surprisingly, they made the trip without too much damage or mishap.

I started working with a real estate agent in Medford and was going out at least three days a week, searching for property. Since we were going out frequently and covering Medford, Jacksonville, Central Point, Eagle Point, Rogue River, Gold River and other outlying areas, I offered to drive my vehicle and save her gas and wear and tear on her car. I also took her to lunch several times. When I didn't find something within the first two weeks, she called me into her office and told me she felt I wasn't ready to make a decision. We had been looking at property on which to place a modular, so the sale would have only been forty to fifty thousand. I guess she felt the commission wouldn't be worth her valuable time. She indicated she wasn't really thrilled about continuing to look, so I started looking on my own. Within the next week, we found the place we would buy, a piece of property with a home already on it. The agent should have persevered. It would have been a much nicer commission.

I had been trying to get Harry to consider the Grants Pass area, but all my efforts received an adamant "No!" He made it quite clear he would not commute to work from Grants Pass to Central Point. Prior to moving here, I had been to Oregon by myself, looking at property in Grants Pass and Merlin, and fell in love with the area, so, after church one Sunday I said, "Let's take a drive. I want to show you this cute little town." We drove around Merlin for a while and were getting ready to leave when we spotted a 'For Sale' sign and information box we had previously missed. The flyer indicated the price had just been reduced. We picked up the flyer Sunday afternoon, looked at the property Tuesday, immediately made an offer, and it was accepted that same day. Harry loved it as much as I did and agreed to commute.

June 14, 2000

Dear Friends and Family,

We finally found a piece of property, made an offer that was accepted, and are now in escrow. The property has an older, modular home on a permanent foundation. It is a double-wide with a large add-on room, extending it to a triple-wide. The extension was very well done, with permits and inspections. Then, the entire mobile and add-on were covered with new siding, so it looks like it was always a part of the original structure. The modular isn't as nice as the new one we were going to purchase, but, with some remodeling, it will be livable and comfortable. We both fell in love with the property.

The property is one and one-third acres, fenced and cross-fenced. It has a well, septic, oversized two-and-a-half-car garage with a large shop area, and a covered RV area in back of the garage, with electrical hook-ups and an RV dump connected to the septic. The back yard is approximately one-half acre of lawn and beautiful, old, shade trees. The front section of the property is approximately one-half acre of pasture, enclosed with white board fencing. The house, front yard and garage sit between the back yard and pasture, on approximately one-third acre. It is a very manicured property that is on a "flag" lot, which means it is in back of another property, rather than on the road. I like that. It is very private. We go down a little lane to get to the property, and the only thing you can see from the road is the garage.

There are three mature apple trees, one pear, one plum and a cherry tree, although the cherry tree doesn't produce anything. All the trees are old and haven't been well-cared-for. Bummer Creek runs through the back of the property, which comprises our property line.

There is a huge satellite dish in the upper pasture. Harry said, "When we get that thing hooked up, you can get about 500 stations."

"Whoopee!" I told him. "For someone (me) who doesn't watch TV, that's a real thrill! Just think. With 500 stations, you could spend the entire evening flipping through the channels, and, at three to five seconds per channel, you'd never get through all the channels and never have to actually watch anything. A perfect evening for a man. Remote control personified!"

(We never did hook up to the satellite, and, eventually, took it down and hauled it to the dump.)

We are now in the process of getting our loan application. If all goes well, we will have a 30- day escrow, to close July 21. That should get us out of this rental by the end of July. We've already given our moving notice. I have to go to Medford tomorrow to take some papers to the lender, so I'd better quit yakking and get this ready to mail. Our love and prayers,

Shirlene and Harry

June 24, 2000

Dear Friends and Family,

When it rained here a couple of weeks ago, I sat on the deck and watched the raindrops dance across the river like a ballerina toe-dancing across a stage. The rain shrouded the mountain- top on the other side of the river in a hazy mist like an elegant lady wearing a shawl. It was a good, soaking rain, and the dry earth absorbed it like a sponge. You could almost see the plants raising thirsty leaves to catch the life-giving moisture. I love the rain, the smell of the fresh-washed earth and grass, and the cool, fresh air. I love snuggling under the covers and listening to it pattering against the roof and windows. I think Oregon and I are going to get along just fine.

As I watched the rain, a lazy duck zoomed down-river, catching a free ride on the swift current. He probably rides the river two or three miles, gets out, flies back up-river and does it all over again. I imagine he is a juvenile duck, using the river as an amusement park ride. *"Wheee! Look Ma, no paddling!"* Well, what are you laughing at? Animals *do* play you know!

One beautiful day recently, I took my laptop to the deck to write letters. We have four giant cottonwood trees out back that are loaded with cotton-ball fluff. A slight breeze came up, and the cottonwood was so thick in the air it looked like snow. The 'snow' was so thick I had to give up and go in the house. Next morning it covered everything with a layer of white. I swept off and hosed down as much as possible, but it was a losing battle. The cottonwood 'snow' lasted for about three weeks, but it is pretty much over now. Thank God! It sure played havoc with my allergies.

Headaches have awakened me the past three mornings in the wee hours of 2:30, 3:30 and 4:30 a.m. I would prefer to sleep until 6:00, but I'm not complaining. It wasn't to be so I am up, sitting on the deck in the pre-dawn lightness, watching and listening to the world wake up.

God is so good! No matter what adversity happens, (even bothersome headaches) He is able to bring something good out of it. If it weren't for the headaches, I wouldn't be up watching the miracle of this day unfold.

Across the river, in this early-dawn darkness, a train goes clickity-clacking by, announcing its presence with a lonely whistle. Soon, it is out of hearing, and only the whistle can be heard, mournfully drifting back in the cool morning air. And the river goes silently on.

Crickets chirp out the last of their night-time melody, fading away to silence as the birds wake up and start looking for breakfast. Suddenly, there is complete quiet—not a sound to break the stillness—as though all the earth is holding its breath, waiting for God's handiwork to unfold. Then the sun tops the ridge of the mountain, and the birds begin their Hallelujah chorus, thanking God for another day. *We* should be so grateful!

A donkey across the river brays good morning, and a couple of geese down-river are having an argument. A resident woodpecker taps out his decision for the winner.

I took Schatze to Medford and had her bathed and clipped. She looks like a totally different dog. During the day when our neighbor is at work, I close the gate to the driveway and let her out of her small dog pen. She streaks around the back yard like a wind-up toy that has gone crazy. I know it must feel good to get out of that small, confining pen and be able to run and get some exercise. Wish I could turn the cats loose. I feel so sorry for them, but if I let them loose, they would be road-kill!

In the early morning, the air is cool enough for a light sweater. My kind of weather. I love it. Later today, it will warm up, but these cool mornings on the deck are such a blessing. God blessed us with this temporary rental on the river, and it has been such a healing balm. Much needed. I'm savoring every minute of these mornings, for we won't be here much longer.

We are now in escrow, and I'm doing the paper-chase game, getting all the documents to the lender. Maybe that's why I'm having headaches, for that process is a real pain in the neck—and other places that shall remain unmentionable!

Merlin is three miles north of Grants Pass, just off I-5. It is the proverbial blink-twice-and-you've-missed-it town, about two blocks long and with a dozen or so stores. Sort of like the town where I grew up.

It occurred to me a few days ago that I have never been completely unpacked and settled, in the six-and-a-half years Harry and I have been married. Seven moves in six-and-a-half years! If Harry even mentions the word "move" to me, he is going to have a very short life span. He has a death wish and I am his fairy Godmother—I can grant his wish! Only God is going to tell me if I have to move again before He takes me home!

Harry asked, "What if my job changes and I have to go somewhere else?"

"Be sure and write," I told him. "What part of *I'm not moving* don't you understand?"

Our new (***permanent***) address will be included on some computer 'business' cards, but don't start using that until I let you know the escrow has closed, so I will know it is really our home. Escrow should close by July 21, but you know how escrows go. They hardly ever close on time. In California, they never closed on time. I don't suppose Oregon will be that much different. It would be nice if it *would* close by July 21. Then, we could be out of here by the first of August, without having to panic about moving in one or two days.

I'm sending a couple of maps (front & back), so you will have an idea where we are located. Only 61 miles north of the California border.

Our next project is to find a better car for Harry, because his old van won't hold up very long with a 60-mile-a-day commute. We hope to find something that gets good gas mileage.

Had best end this 'gab' session. Will keep you posted as things progress. And, thanks to those of you who have written. Since I'm up here away from all my friends and family, it is really nice to get a letter.

Wishing you God's blessings,

Shirlene and Harry

June 26, 2000

Dear Friends and Family,

Another morning on the deck at 5:30, enjoying the refreshing coolness. How I love this early morning time! I never see the resident woodpecker that lives down-river, but I hear him at this time every morning. I think he believes that his rat-a-tat-tat is chasing away the darkness and bringing on the sun. And who knows? He may be right, for soon after he begins his Morse code, sunlight streaks through the trees and across the river. Confident that he has accomplished his task for the morning, he is silent—until tomorrow, when he will again call the sun up over the mountain.

Two ducks were squawking on the river, and they sounded very close. I could hear them, but couldn't see them, so I tiptoed onto the top deck. They sounded like they were verrry close, but I still couldn't see them, so, very quietly, I made my way down the steps to the lower deck. The sound was closer, but still no ducks in sight. I leaned over the deck railing, and at that moment, they erupted from the weeds at the water's edge directly beneath me. It's a good thing there is a railing around that deck, or I would have fallen in the river. I think the drake was telling sweet lies to his lady love, and he wasn't too happy that I had interrupted. Neither was she, for they both gave me a verbal quacking as they flew away. Sure glad I can't understand duck language, for I think there may have been some name-calling in there.

The little bird that was rejected by all the females is still around, squawking his agonizing cry from 4:30 a.m. until about 6:00. If I could get my hands on that fractured, feathered friend while he's squawking out his discordant operetta, I'd wring his scrawny neck and put him out of his misery. . . and mine! Harry said, "I never knew there were birds that couldn't sing!" Neither did I, but this one definitely can't. I've named him Harry!

The sun is up, highlighting the mountain across the river, and a circling hawk, searching for breakfast, squeals his hunting cry. It seems strange to hear a hawk this close to civilization, but it is not the hawk that has moved into civilized territory, but humans that have moved in on the hawk. Perhaps, his cry is the same as that of the Indians—just go away and leave me alone to live my life in peace. But, we will no more leave the hawk his hunting territory than we did the Indians. Where there used to be bare mountains, now they are decorated with houses, encroaching farther and farther into the hawk, bear and deer's domain. The hawk squeals again, and there is a lonely appeal to his cry, but it is ignored, as man starts his heavy equipment to clear off space for another house.

The Indians believed we are one with the earth and brothers with the animals, that we are only keepers and have a responsibility to live with the earth without destroying it. They were right, and we reap the results of our chemical destruction on a daily basis, with all of our illnesses and disease, for we have destroyed God's balance.

The ducks have returned below the decks, but I will leave them alone, as his arduous quacking is becoming more insistent. "Oh, please, honey! It will clear your complexion!!"

As the weather gets hotter, there are more and more rafters on the river, and they are driving that poor, yellow Lab across the river to distraction. He stands on the bank and warns them not to come near his side of the water. I'll bet this river will be full of rafters on the fourth of July, and that Lab will be a basket-case with a sore throat by the end of the day. Yesterday, he was in the water, swimming. When the other dog followed their master back up the bank out of the water, the lab stayed and swam until his master got rather insistent about him getting out.

I once knew a man who had a black Lab that couldn't swim and was afraid of the water. He said, "Labs are suppose to be water dogs and this dumb-cluck can't swim." We were laughing, but, he said, "I'm serious. I decided one time to make him swim, so I threw him in the water. I had to jump in and save him, because he almost drowned."

I let Schatze out of her pen for an evening run. Look out yard bugs! The great hunter is loose! Wish I could let the cats out. They have been cooped up in that small 8' x 12' pen for a month now. They have another month to go before the escrow closes, and we can move to our home. Then, they'll be able to roam free.

And, another month before I will feel free. I hate renting. I can't hang paintings (might make holes in the wall); can't put up shelves, or change the wall paper, or plant anything. I can sympathize with the cats because I also feel really confined. If we had to rent, this house on the river was a good spot. Still, it isn't home. After owning my own home for the past 24 years, renting is the pits. Soon it will be over. One more month!

Keep us in your prayers. You are in ours,

Shirlene and Harry

July 4, 2000

D ear Friends and Family,

I started this, but didn't get it finished and in the mail, due to an unwanted intrusion. I got sick! I mean really sick. I think I got salmonella. I was sick all night, and when Harry finally woke up, I had him take me to emergency. I was very dehydrated, so they put me on an IV and gave me some medication to stop the vomiting. The doctor explained that they didn't usually give antibiotics with this type of thing, unless there is bacteria. I said, "Fine, I don't like to take antibiotics." He came back with two prescriptions—one for nausea and vomiting, the other, antibiotics. There *was* bacteria, which is a sign of salmonella. I took the stuff the first day, then decided I was feeling better, so I didn't take it yesterday. By late afternoon, I was getting sick again, so I'm back on the medication, feeling better, and this time I will stay on it until it is finished.

I had a pleasant surprise when I got back from the hospital Saturday. There was a message from some friends, with whom I had gone to church, when I previously lived in Oregon (a couple of centuries ago.) My friends now live in Redmond, about a four-and-a-half hour drive from here, and they wanted to come to see us on Monday. I was too sick to return the call, so I went to bed and slept for the remainder of the day. Around 5:30, I called them. Although we've kept in touch by mail, it has been years since I've seen them, so I said, "Come on over, we'd love to have you." I didn't tell them I had been sick all night or that I'd been in Emergency.

They came and spent the night, and we had such a wonderful visit. Karen said, "Why didn't you tell me you were sick? We wouldn't have come."

"I know. That's why I didn't tell you. I wasn't about to miss this visit." What a blessing to have good friends. If God has blessed me with any riches in this lifetime, it is with the wealth of people I have as friends. Most of the time I'm not sure why my friends put up with me, but God bless each one of them for their patience and endurance.

Only eighteen more days until MD (moving day,)—IF the escrow closes on time—but then, who's counting? I'm dreading the move and looking forward to it at the same time. Each move has seemed to get worse than the previous one, but, I keep telling myself it can't possibly be as bad as the last one. How's that for being a perpetual optimist?! The escrow is to close on the 21st. Pray that it does. If it doesn't close, we may be floating down river on our furniture, for we've already given our notice here.

Today has been the quietest 4th of July I've ever experienced. I thought the river would be full of rafters (haven't seen a soul). From the sound of firecrackers going off all week long, I figured we were in for a noisy day. (Haven't heard *one* firecracker.) I think they must have used them all up before the holiday got here. That's okay. Quiet is what I like best!

July 5, 2000

I awoke to a gentle summer rain, whispering a lullaby against the metal shed outside my window. The rain, light as goose down, left a mist that sat on top of the mountain. In the distance, black trees danced in and out of the mist, playing hide-and-seek. The rain tip-toed on by and the sun peeked through the clouds, like a shy child peeking around its mother's skirts, only to duck back when noticed. I sat on the deck with my breakfast and breathed in the fresh-washed air, my lungs saying "thank you."

If my addle-pated brain doesn't get sidetracked before I get this sealed and in the mail, I will include a card with our new address and phone number—not to be used until after close of escrow! Harry thinks these cards are silly, and didn't want his name on them, but they come in handy for me when I'm at some place of business and they say, "Let me have your name and phone number." I just hand them a card. I do them on the computer, so when I run out, I make a new batch.

Not much else to write, so I'll close. Hope you are well.

Our love and prayers,

Shirlene and Harry

July 12, 2000

Dear Friends and Family,

Our escrow is scheduled to close in a few days and things are getting very busy and hectic. (what else is new?) I talked to the loan officer today, and she said everything was approved in underwriting. All they need now is Harry's job verifications from Arizona, and Rotary Rocket in Southern California, then they can order the documents and close, possibly even a day or two early. That would surely be a blessing.

You probably won't hear from me for three or four weeks while I'm in the packing-moving-unpacking-sorting mess. I can't wait to get started and get it over with.

One of the first things we plan on doing is tearing out and remodeling the old kitchen. I've already ordered my new appliances, but haven't ordered the cabinets yet. I have to wait until the cabinet people can get here to take measurements. It takes about four weeks for the cabinets to be made, then shipped, and it will take at least that long for Harry to install them, working just weekends and evenings. It looks like we'll be camping out and maybe cooking hotdogs on a camp stove for a couple of months. That's going to be fun when it rains.

We bought our garden/lawn tractor last week and have already moved it to the property. No point in moving it to the rental and having to move it again. Harry has already put it to use. New toy!

The Merlin Post Office has been notified of our upcoming move, so it is all right to use our new address at this point. Since the property is vacant, and we have the seller's permission, I will be out there prior to the move, cleaning carpets and getting everything ready to move in. I met one of our neighbors today, a teenage boy named Brian, and hired him and his brother, Jason, to help with our move.

Much to do in the next couple of weeks, but everything is going so smoothly I know God has cleared the way.

Our love and prayers,

Shirlene and Harry

July 17, 2000

Dear Friends and Family,

Well, some people have bats in the belfry, we have birds in the chimney—and living room. A few weeks ago, a couple of Swallows built a nest in the chimney. We knew they were building it because once or twice they lost their sense of direction and flew into the fireplace. The glass doors to the fireplace were closed and, after several attempts to get out that way, they found their way up and out. Two or three weeks later, we heard soft chirp-chirping and knew the babies had hatched. As they grew, the chirping became more incessant and louder, and it went on allll day and sometimes until 10:00 o'clock at night.

I was concerned that the young birds might have a problem when they were ready to fly. Unfortunately, I was right. Yesterday, a baby bird dropped down inside the fireplace and couldn't get back out. The problem is, our glass-doored fireplace has a U-shaped inset of pipes that extend from the bottom, up the back and over the top, to circulate the heat. Once inside the fireplace, the babies can't get back up because of the overhead pipes. They were trying to get out the glass doors, and I was afraid they would hurt themselves, so I opened the doors before I went to bed. When I got up this morning, there were three baby birds in the living room. I caught them and gently eased them up the side of the fireplace and put them on top of the pipes, in the hope they would be able to fly upward and get out. No such luck. I spent most of the day putting baby birds back on top of the pipes, only to have them drop back down again. The parents would not come down the chimney far enough to feed the birds, and the babies could not get back up the chimney, so they weren't getting any nourishment and were getting listless. Finally, we put one of them on the roof. It immediately flew off the roof into the nearest tree. We are waiting for the others to drop down again so we can put them outside, hoping the parents will return. The second little one we put on the roof probably won't make it. It was completely covered with soot, even inside its mouth, and when we put it on the roof, it just stayed there. Poor baby! I hope the rest make it, but since they haven't been fed today, and the parents don't seem to be coming back, they may not.

I notified the property management people that they should put a screen across the top of the chimney. Otherwise, the next hatchling of birds won't have anyone to release them, and they will die inside the fireplace.

We've had several days of hot, humid, overcast weather, but no rain. Most of the clouds have cleared up, but the few remaining on the western horizon are a most beautiful shade of peach, tinted with lavender-gray against a soft blue sky, back-dropping a green mountain. I love this time of day when the sun has hidden behind the mountain. It is still light, but the day is reluctant to end, like a sleepy child, fighting to stay awake.

Our escrow should have all the paperwork completed in the morning and will close tomorrow afternoon or early Wednesday. I'm amazed that it is closing a couple of days early, but I really shouldn't be because God's hand has been in this from the beginning. Everything seems to be falling in place. The new appliances I ordered for the kitchen remodeling will be delivered this Saturday. Harry will be stripping the old carpet out of the den on Saturday and getting it prepped for the new carpet to be installed on Tuesday. I will be moving boxes from this house to our new home most of next week, and the following Saturday, the 29th, we will be moving our furniture. We have to have everything out of here and this placed cleaned and ready for inspection by the 31st. We'll keep you posted.

Our love and prayers,

Shirlene and Harry

August 9, 2000

Dear Friends & Family,

It rained early this morning. Not enough to do much good, just wet the top half-inch of soil, but it was nice while it lasted. It rained, stopped, started, stopped, started for about thirty minutes. I stood on the front porch and watched it, reveling in the cool air. Alas, it didn't last. The sun came out and pretty soon everything was hot and steamy. It has been a hot day.

Now it is evening, and the clouds are rolling back into the area, ushered in by drum rolls of thunder, accented with lightning. All that pomp and ceremony but no action. Perhaps we'll get a good rain this evening. We surely could use it.

Harry has been installing a utility tub in our laundry room. He ignored Ol' Man Thunder's warning and set his saw up just outside the garage doors, and now it is sprinkling on the saw. Not really raining, just sprinkling enough to make muddy messes on the pickup windshield.

I was in hopes it would rain enough this morning to soften the ground in the pasture, so I could get some of the teasel, star thistle and blackberry vines dug out, but it didn't happen. I dug some of them out with a shovel, but I think a jack-hammer would have worked better. This ground is decomposed lava rock, and sometimes I don't think it is very "*de*-composed." It's harder than making snake-eyes on a dice roll! I think it may take several years of composted organic matter to get this ground to produce a garden.

I have been pricing cabinets this week, in an effort to get the kitchen remodeling started. I can't really unpack and get settled in until the kitchen is complete, so we are camping out and living out of boxes. What else is new? I haven't been completely unpacked in the six-and-a-half years we've been married! The cabinet prices are ranging from "ridiculous" to "ouch, that hurt!" I'm hoping to go somewhere in between the two.

My goofy little dog chose this time to come into season. I haven't been able to find a breeder in Oregon, so I will have to take her to Nevada City, California, this Saturday, leave her with the breeder and drive back home on Sunday. Then, next weekend, I get to repeat the process to pick her up. I'm not looking forward to two weekends of driving, but there isn't much choice. If she has puppies, they should be born in October, ready for sale around the middle of December. Christmas puppies! I'll run an ad in Sacramento to sell them. Down there, they sell like hotcakes. This will be her first litter, so she will probably only have two or three, and the breeder gets pick of the litter.

After being locked up in an 8' x 12' dog run for two months, my cats were scared to death the first two days I turned them loose. They ran off and hid. After the second day, curiosity overcame fear, and they started wandering out of the garage and exploring. A whole acre and a third to roam, play hide-and-seek, and hunt. They love it.

For all the thunder and lightning we have had, we certainly didn't get any waterworks to speak of. The clouds have mostly passed on by, and the ones on the tail end of the cloud bank have turned a lovely lavender-gray in the setting sun. It is so pretty here, so peaceful. My neighbor, Jo, who lives in front of us by the road, calls this "a little piece of heaven on earth." She has moved twenty-nine times in her lifetime and lived in a lot of different areas, so I think her comment is fairly well-qualified.

I happened to glance out the window and saw a beautiful, pink rainbow piercing through the lavender and gray clouds, against a pale blue sky, sitting on top of tall, green pine trees. Although the sun has not yet set, the moon is already up and is dancing through holes in the clouds. Absolutely beautiful!

There is a hole in the fence separating our property and the neighbor on the south side. They have two big dogs that stand at the fence with their heads poked through the hole, barking hello at me whenever I'm outside. They wait, tails wagging, for me to come to the fence and give them a dog biscuit. Don't yet know the names of my "fence peekers," but we're friends anyway.

Jo, our neighbor on the east side, has a horse named Romeo. She says he is a love, and I believe it. Today, when I was digging up thistle in our pasture, he came to the fence to get acquainted. So far, all my neighbors and their animals have been friendly. I haven't yet met Jo's Greyhound, King, but the German Shepard, Sabrina, is a sweetheart.

We are gradually getting acquainted at the Merlin Community Baptist Church where we have been attending. I am thrilled they will have a women's Bible study, starting in September. I've certainly missed the Bible study I attended in Southern California. I do my own Bible study at home and will continue to do so, but I miss the fellowship and input of other Christians, and of course, it is a good way to get acquainted and establish friendships. I'm so thankful for God's guidance in directing us to this area, this home and this church. When His hand is upon something, it really comes together. He never ceases to amaze me.

It is almost 9:00 p.m.—that dusky time of evening when lights are being turned on, but it is still light enough outside to see everything. A few straggling clouds are trying to catch up with the main bank that has already passed on through, and the white moon, looking like a marshmallow with a bite taken out of it, keeps wandering in and out of the clouds. It is the time of evening that is sprinkled with fairy dust, a magic that lasts only a few fleeting minutes and is gone.

I suppose I should be going also. Morning will get here sooner than I want, and there is much to accomplish tomorrow, so I will say good night.

God bless and keep you until next time,

Shirlene and Harry

It would be impossible for me to include letters from various friends and family members, however, one of my most treasured letters, from my son-in-law, was answered prayer and has a special place in my heart, so I felt it should be a part of this diary.

August 15, 2000

Mom and Harry,

I'm so happy to know that you have found such a beautiful home. I can hardly wait to visit and confirm that the pictures didn't "come with the frame." Congratulations. The Lord willing, we're next!

I hoped that we would be able to make a trip prior to Brantley starting school but it doesn't appear that is going to happen. There was, however, a story in the paper the other day regarding her teachers and the status of their on-going efforts to reach an agreement. Although they received a retro payment of wages, they did not receive the new contract they were seeking. It appears to me they will be back on strike shortly after the school year begins. So. . .God may be working His magic after all. Not only would the kids enjoy seeing you both, but I have located a couple of B&B's that have our names on them. Quality time with Grandma/Grandpa for the kids, coupled with locating a lost-in-the-clutter "lust" for one another would do Kelly and I a world of good.

Our vacation was without incident, which, all things considered, may be the best comment possible. It wasn't that we didn't enjoy ourselves, but Brantley and Parker certainly ran the show. I know that I probably had that much energy at their age, but it appears to have left me along with the memories of it. I'm not old enough yet! All kidding aside, we did enjoy Vegas and the promise of a return trip, one better planned, as well as the time with my sister and future brother-in-law, Brian.

As I'm sure Kelly has mentioned, I am enjoying my walk with Jesus more and more everyday. Although the path has turned away many times to this point in my life, I know the "Y's" are becoming less extreme. Although I have not said anything directly to you in the past, you must know that I hold a very special place in my heart for the influence you have had on me. Your work as a disciple of His Word has not fallen on deaf ears, empty heart or mind.

We had the pleasure of standing before the congregation this past Sunday in offering ourselves, Brantley and Parker at the church's quarterly Child Dedication. Your prayers in support of us becoming better Christian parents, leading our children to know Jesus and the power of a relationship with Him, would be greatly appreciated. Kelly will be forwarding the insert from the church's bulletin soon.

I can't think of a better ending. Much love and I look forward to doing this more often!

Derek

August 17, 2000

Dear Derek,

I just went to the post office and mailed a "family" letter to you and Kelly, and of course, letters to my two favorite little people in all the world. Then I got your beautiful letter out of the mailbox, and it just made my day—my week—my month—my year!! Well, you get the idea. It was really sweet of you to write, as I really enjoy hearing from people, but the *content* of the letter is what really thrilled my heart.

Actually, Kelly hasn't said much about where you are in your spiritual life, so I am thrilled that you wrote to me. I, too, am enjoying my walk with Jesus more each day. There is a song that says, "It's sweeter, as the days go by," and I couldn't agree more. My main regret is that I wasted so many years before I really found Jesus and understood what He expected of me. I'm still learning, but at least now, I am studying and understanding more, and with that understanding comes a peace and joy that is found nowhere else. Money won't buy it, and success and fame won't acquire it.

My own path turned away many times, and it took me more years to find Christ than it has taken you. I spent many years being a Sunday morning bench warmer, and doing my own thing the rest of the week. Didn't work, doesn't work, never will work! One Sunday on the way home from Church—right in the middle of a Western song I was listening to—God gave me a warning. *Be ye either hot or cold or I will spew you out of my mouth!* I knew it was from God, because it certainly wasn't something I was thinking at the time. I went home and looked up the verse. It isn't worded exactly as He gave it to me, but the meaning is the same. Rev 3:15-16 *15 I know thy works that thou art neither hot nor cold.*[16] *So then because thou art lukewarm and neither cold nor hot, I will spew you out of my mouth*. That was me—lukewarm! That's when I made the decision to turn my life, my *whole* life, over to God, and I've never regretted it. Oh, I still make mistakes, still stumble and fall on my posterior end, and I'm sure God must shake His head in exasperation at my failures; but thankfully, He is a loving, forgiving God, so He picks me up, dusts me off and says, "Try again, and this time, do it better." I'll never get it perfect until I stand in His presence, made perfect in Him, but I'll keep trying. As long as I'm trying and growing, I know I'll be covered by His grace. Thank God for grace!

One of the things that has helped me the most is studying His word with the *Thru The Bible* series. I left one of the books, beginning with Matthew, Mark, etc., in the New Testament, at your house. If you have any questions about scripture, go look it up in there. Old Vernon McGee sure makes it easy to understand, verse by verse.

Wish I could have been there when you made your commitment at church, but rest assured, dear one, that you are daily in my prayers and have been for the past ten years. I will never stop praying for all of you, as long as I am alive. In Paul's gospel, he admonished us to pray for one another, and it is the best thing we could possibly do. Yes, I pray all the time that my grandchildren will be led to Christ. I also pray for your mother, dad and sister, and for many of my own family members who are not saved, although some of them would be furious if they knew. Doesn't matter. God knows. Sometimes, our prayers take years to be answered, but God does hear. He just never forces people. We all have to make our own choices.

If there should be an opportunity for you to come to visit, we would love to have you. You and Kelly can have my room (so you'll have some privacy) and the kids and I will take the living room. There are so many pretty areas to see in this state, and we'd love to have the kids while you and Kelly have some private time. You need it.

Glad your vacation turned out all right and without problems. Too bad you can't bottle and sell Brantley and Parker's energy. You'd be instant millionaires! And I'd be the first in line to buy a bottle!

Our remodeling is started but going slowly. Harry works long hours and doesn't have very much time to work on things here, although he certainly makes the effort. He comes home every night and works until almost bedtime. So many projects! Oh, well, it will just take time to get everything done. The major thing is the kitchen, and from the looks of things, that won't be finished until October. It takes six to eight weeks to get the cabinets after they have been ordered, and we haven't ordered them yet.

Harry will be home soon and I must start dinner, so I'll close and thank you again for your letter. No matter what you are doing, or where you are, always know that I am praying for you.

Much love,

Mom

August 19, 2000

Dear Friends and Family,

The previous owners of this home had the foresight to install electrical plugs on the back deck, which certainly makes it convenient for me to sit out here with my computer, watching the sun play hide-and-seek with a straggle of clouds and listening to the wind sighing through the trees, hinting of the end of summer. It has gone so quickly! Oh, we're still having warm days and using the air conditioner, but the evening breeze has the tiniest change in it, warning of cooler days. "Sooon, sooon," it seems to say.

Harry mowed our huge, back lawn last night and part of the pasture, and finished it today. He likes that riding lawn mower. Sort of like a back-yard cowboy. I think I heard him say, "Giddy- up!"

When the back yard is mowed, it looks like a park. It will look even better after we get rid of those tenacious blackberries, but that won't be until sometime next summer. Can't afford it right now, with all the remodeling we have to do. I don't know if you can ever really get rid of blackberries because the roots go all the way to China. I suspect some alien space ship landed here and planted blackberries to take over the world—and it's working! Even though I don't like having to fight all the plants and runners, the berries have been good. We both go out every day, stand and pick berries and eat our fill. I've managed to put a few in the freezer, but most of them just go in our mouths.

An ad in the Nickel paper said, "Free guineas. Insect and snake control. You catch." Did you ever try to catch a guinea? Ha! It's not like catching chickens. These birds are evasively smart and can fly quite well, thank you. I drove to Applegate Valley, and the lady who had the guineas, and I, armed with our fishing nets, were prepared to do battle. We were outfoxed and outflanked from the get-go. The guineas were in the barn, so Janet closed the barn door, and we slipped inside. Unfortunately, her barn is the kind that has a roof that drops down about four feet from the top; then, there is about a twelve inch gap for air circulation, and the second part of the roof starts under the eves of the first section. The guineas took one look at us with our silly fish nets and flew up to the opening in the roof. Before we could get the barn doors open and get outside, they dropped down off the roof into the tall grass and disappeared, laughing all the way.

Janet said she would put some food in a dog carrier and see if she could catch them that way. A couple of days later, she called and said she caught one, so I drove back to Applegate Valley, about a 70-mile round trip, and transferred the one guinea from her dog carrier to mine. I gave it food and water and let it stay in the dog carrier the rest of the day and all night. The next morning, I turned it loose, hoping it would stay. It eeeped and chirped its way across the yard, disappeared into the blackberry brambles, and I haven't seen it since. I guess you could say my "chicken" flew the coop! Somewhere along the creek, among the blackberries and bushes, is a wild, free-roaming guinea singing, *Don't Fence Me In.*

Next spring when I buy my baby chickens, I'll buy some guineas and raise them from keets. Hopefully, they will then stay on the property. They eat things like earwigs, deer ticks, miscellaneous other insects and they get rid of snakes. I especially appreciate the last part.

The sun has gone down, the crickets are serenading, and the wind has a chill in it, promising that fall is coming, so I will pack up my laptop and go inside where a nice cup of tea is begging to be brewed. Don't go far away. We'll visit more later.

August 22, 2000

Hello, again! It is *now* later than you think! Did you miss me? Schatze is still in Sacramento, and I'm sitting here waiting for the breeder to call me to come and get her. Don't know what is taking so long. Maybe Schatze just decided she didn't want to have puppies.

On Sunday, we decided to drive from here to the coast, which is only 75 miles. An hour-and-a-half or two-hour drive, right? **Wrong!** The road, Hwy 23, going out of Galice and coming out at Gold Beach, is one of the worst I have ever been on. We went over the mountains, and I do mean *over* the mountains, right across the top. The road was an old logging road that hasn't been updated. In most parts, it was one lane, although it was open to two lane traffic. Narrow and twisting, with heart-stopping drop-offs. Parts of the road had washed away during the last rains, and on five different sections we were driving on gravel. The parts that hadn't washed away had cracked and sunk down six inches to a foot, giving a definite sense of adventure to drive across. Most people we met were good about pulling off at the nearest wide spot, except one jerk (there always has to be one, doesn't there?) The turn-out was on his side, and we were too far across to do anything but proceed. No turn-out on our side, just a sheer drop off. He passed his turn off and crowded on by. I thought surely he was going to push us over the edge. We passed each other with only inches between us. Would you believe I won't be going to the coast by that road, ever again? The trip took us three-and-a-half hours! Needless to say, we drove *up* the coast and came home on Hwy. 42 to Roseburg. Good road all the way.

We got to Gold Beach so late that we didn't have much time for "walking on the beach." It was just as well because the wind was blowing, it was colder than an Eskimo's nose, and neither of us took a jacket. When I was getting ready to go, I told myself to remember to take a jacket, but by the time I got dressed and gathered up other paraphernalia, I forgot about the coat. I have a colander mind—everything just sifts right through the holes!

We were almost starved when we finally got to Gold Beach, so we had lunch around 2:00 p.m. at a little place called The Hole In The Wall. Great food and plenty of it, but I won't tell you it was worth the drive over that mountain road.

(Note: The road herein described has been in the National news, as it has since claimed several lives, especially if people try to cross it in winter. It is not maintained and should be avoided!)

I suppose I'd better quit writing and get busy. There's enough work around here to last me until the next millennium. If you haven't anything to do, come to visit. I'll put you to work.

Our love and prayers,

Shirlene and Harry

September 1, 2000

Dear Friends and Family,

September already! The last few days of August the weather cooled and hinted that fall was just around the corner, and as an appropriate end to the month, it sprinkled. Today the clouds have been teasingly promising rain but, like politicians, so far have failed to produce. While I was outside, two or three raindrops blop-plopped on my head. Either that, or we had some low-flying birds. I was afraid to put my hand on my head to find out which! Some things are better not known. Anyway, it never did rain. Maybe tonight. . . .

I love the changing seasons. I guess spring would be my favorite season, so welcome with everything coming to life again. But, fall holds a close second. The hot weather cools off enough to be soothingly pleasant, and the trees dress up in their fall finery. The tops of our blue mountains are snuggled under a quilt of white, goose-down clouds, and the breeze scatters dry leaves to be composted for next year's flowers and vegetables. Geese are beginning to fly over, honking their exodus. The male in front is honking, "Follow me girls!" while the geese are honking back, "You fool, you're going the wrong way! Stop at that Exxon and ask directions." (He's a male. He won't stop.)

Harry has the divider wall between the den and sewing room almost finished, and I bought new ceiling lights to install. Every room in this house will have *some* remodeling done to it by the time we are through—*if* we are ever through. (Are we having fun yet?)

I went to the post office to pick up some Iris bulbs I ordered, and a couple of 9-10-year-old kids outside the post office were selling squash. Most of the other adults said a polite "No, thank you," and passed on by, but they caught me. I swear, I must have some sort of mark on my forehead that says, "Here comes number one-sucker! She'll buy." This mark is not visible to adults, only to children. I know they've had my house marked for years, just like the hobos used to mark houses during the depression, only my house mark says, "Hey, kids! This way for any project you want supported." Oh, well. One of the best investments we can make is in children, so I figure it's for a good cause.

The two dogs next door, Misty and Foxy, put their heads through the hole in the fence every night and "wuf, wuf," at me, for their dog-bone treat. I think that mark on my forehead is also visible to animals.

A shelf, eighteen-inches wide and eight-feet long, in back of the garage under the RV roof, has been designated as the cat's feeding area. The shelf is about four-feet off the ground and holds cat food, dog food, feeding dishes and cat carriers, where the cat's often sleep. The food is safe from the dog when she is out, and the cats can easily jump onto the shelf when they are hungry. However, when I go out just before dark to feed them their canned cat food, they both gather around my feet and meow for me to lift them onto the shelf. A four-foot jump is nothing for these two. They jump up there all the time. They want me to lift them up, simply because they want my attention. Spoiled cats!

Last night when I went out to feed, they were rubbing against my ankles, meowing to be lifted up. Harry was passing by so he picked up the little one (C.C.—Compact Cat) and put her on the shelf. She gave him a really dirty look (yes, cats can do that) that said, "Butt out, Buddy. You're messing up my act." Then, she jumped off the shelf, looked up at me helplessly and meowed pitifully to be picked up. What a con artist!

September 2, 2000

I awoke around 3:15 a.m. with the rain playing soft lullabies on the roof. I snuggled under the covers with the rain singing to me and went back to sleep, smiling. It's still raining, a soft steady rain that soaks the dry land. In spite of summer-long watering, sections of the lawn dry out and die, but as soon as God starts watering, the dead-looking grass resurrects and turns green. It never ceases to amaze me how He brings life out of dead seeds, grasses and bulbs. What is even more amazing is that he brings eternal life to *us*, who are dead in sin. Christ said, "*....except a corn of wheat fall into the ground and die, it abideth alone: but if it die, it bringeth forth much fruit.*" John

12:24. When we admit we are sinners and die to sin, the blood he shed on the cross washes and cleanses us, and He resurrects us to eternal life with Him. Amazing!

The rain has temporarily stopped, but the gray mantle hangs on, hiding the mountains from view. The rain isn't over, it is just taking a break, and so will I.

September 7, 2000

Long break! Consider this an addendum, because I just keep adding on.

I bought the skylights August 31st, and Harry now has the kitchen skylight installed. The two smaller ones will have to wait. Harry was going to install them this past weekend, but postponed it because of predicted rain. About the time he gets a hole cut in the roof, the skies will open up, and we don't have flood insurance.

The ceiling lights are now installed in the den and sewing room, and the kitchen cabinets are ordered. We should receive them in four to six weeks, so we are looking at the end of September or the middle of October.

Harry is digging out one of the planter beds for my Irises, and I am plotting areas for planting fruit trees and about 200-plus tulips, daffodils, lilies, freesia and hyacinths. Before planting my bulbs, we have to dig out an area and line it with wire to keep the gophers from eating the bulbs, which they consider to be hors d'oeuvres. I hope they break a tooth on the wire.

I also have roses, geraniums, Echinacia and a few miscellaneous plants to put in the ground. I will set out a few lavender plants, but will wait until next spring to start my herb garden.

The apples and pears in the old orchard are now ready to pick. They are small but good tasting, and they will make good applesauce. The trees appear to have been neglected for several years, for they are in dire need of pruning. If we prune them this fall while they are dormant, and thin the fruit next spring, we should have a much better crop next year.

I used the garden tractor last night for the first time and mowed our back and front lawns. It isn't hard to do, just time consuming because there is so much of it (about a half acre). I'll try to keep it up from now on and take some of the extra work off Harry. I can't work outside in the sun because the doctor says I will get skin cancer (from a previous second degree burn about seven years ago), so I use the last couple of hours before dark and actually get quite a lot accomplished in that time frame. I still have to paint the fence before we get into heavy, rainy weather. One thing about living here, there is always something to do. Actually, I've always stayed busy, so there have been very few times in my life when I have been bored. I've just never had time to be bored.

We plan on installing a wood stove for heating, after the kitchen is completed, (yet another project!) so, yesterday I found one and put it on hold. It is a Waterford, (yes, the same company that makes Waterford crystal), made in Ireland. It is a really pretty stove with a green porcelain finish, and a glass front. I love the wood heat and, as our house is all electric, a wood stove will be a real life-saver when the electricity goes out. (This is Oregon—the electricity *will* go out.) We'll have heat, can cook a pot of stew, and have a cup of hot tea.

I found a really ugly black beetle, about an inch-and-a-half long, by the garage. I killed it. I was telling Harry about it, and he said, "Did it have a horn on top of its head? That kind is a rhino beetle."

"Well, I didn't know what kind it was until after I killed it."

"Oh. What kind was it?"

"**Dead** beetle!" I informed him.

I'll sure be glad to get some kind of barn or shed built this winter so I can get my chickens and guineas, and they can clean up this property. As soon as they are raised, I'm going to point them toward the bugs and say, "sic 'em!"

September 8, 2000

I went out today and looked at Nigerian Dwarf goats. They are so cute! Of course, I can't get them for a while, until we get a proper, escape-proof pen, but perhaps in a couple of months, after the kitchen is finished. Maybe they can get rid of all the blackberries at the back of the property.

When I got home, there was a call on the recorder, telling me our cabinets will be delivered October 4th. Hooray! I told Harry the cabinets will be here in three weeks, so he will have to quit goofing around and get busy. He just went down the hall, laughing hysterically.

Hoping this finds you in God's grace. Our love and prayers,

Shirlene and Harry

September 18, 2000

D ear Friends and Family,

Just when I thought we were getting a hint of fall, the weather has turned hot again. It was eighty degrees *inside* today, so I know it must have been eighty-five to ninety degrees outside. I stayed inside (most of the day) with the air conditioner running. I usually wait until around 5:30 or 6:00 in the evening before going outside to work. By that time, the big shade trees and our tall garage have shaded most of the yard, and, usually, a nice breeze is fanning the trees. We've had a few cloudy days, but no rain. It must have rained in the surrounding mountains, though, because our creek is up a little bit.

We've had *something* going through the yard at night, tearing open bags of dog food, cat food and bird food, not eating much of anything except cat food, just wasting and scattering the rest. I bought some barrels with lids and put all the food in covered containers. The cats have howled a few times at night like the very devil was after them, so I've been locking them in the garage in the evening and letting them out the next morning. They seem happy to get inside, so I guess they realize it's for their safety.

This past weekend, Harry worked on taking the kitchen apart, and still has to take off some of the old wall board. When this unit was built, back in the '80's, everything was being "interior decorated" in harvest gold, orange and brown. Not exactly my favorite colors. This one had 1/4" wallpapered, wall board in the kitchen, in nutmeg, rust and tan. Evidently the original owners didn't like that, so they requested a wallpaper pattern in yellow and brown. The manufacturer just put the second wall board over the first, so Harry is now tearing out two sets instead of one. Unfortunately, the second one was just as ugly as the first. The next owner didn't like that pattern, so they *painted* over it with white paint. All the cupboards are particle board and falling apart. Need I explain why I want a complete new kitchen?

I asked Harry to save as much of the wall board as possible, so we can put it in the chicken coop when we build it. I don't think the chickens will mind the colors, and it will help keep out the drafts. With the inside of the chicken coop having wallpapered paneling, I'm going to have the snootiest, high-class chickens in the neighborhood! Well, cock-a-doodle-dooo!

Where Harry has removed all the wall board between the kitchen and living room wall, we can now walk between the 2' x 4's to get from one room to the other. Talk about your open floor plans! There are still more wall boards to be removed, plumbing has to be moved and re-installed, and new wiring. Right now, we have electrical wiring hanging from the ceiling with light switches and plugs dangling at the ends.

The cabinets will be here in two weeks, probably another two weeks to get them installed, since Harry can only work on them part-time, so we are looking at probably another month or more before we have a kitchen. I no longer have an oven, but Harry moved the built-in range top to the 2' x 4' wall in the living room, so I can still cook. Looks lov-erly!—how many people have a cook stove top in their living room? Do you get the impression this man likes his home-cooked meals?

The cooking range is in the living room, and the refrigerator is still in the almost-gutted-out kitchen. We are washing dishes and getting our water from the wash tub in the laundry room, and my only counter-top work space is the dining room table. Trying to run back and forth among the four areas to cook something is a big joke. Also, a big pain in the. . . neck. I considered getting roller blades, but I don't think they would work very well on carpet. Some people have Early American interior decorating, some have Scandinavian, Modern, Antique or European. Me? I have "Perpetual Remodeling!"

From the looks of things, the breeding of Schatze was a wash-out, so no puppies. I view that with mixed emotions. The money would have been nice, but I don't need the extra hassles right now. Oh, well. Easy come, easy go! With the critters and creatures that wander through here at night, what we really need is a big dog, but I can't do anything in that area until we get a gate. Another project.

Schatze's dog pen is the fruit orchard. When the apples started falling, she picked up one and tossed it in the air like a ball. In the process of playing with it, she discovered it was sweet. Now we see her selecting an apple and lying down to eat the whole thing. The apples won't hurt her. In fact, they are probably good for her, but I don't know many dogs that like apples. Crazy little dog.

I picked a bucket of apples and a smaller bucket of pears today. Most of the fruit is worm-infested from lack of care, but I think I found enough apples for applesauce. The ones I picked today were Yellow Delicious, but the Rome Beauty apples are beginning to ripen. Maybe, we'll get a few of those that aren't wormy. The pears are Bartlett, and the few we found without damage have had wonderful flavor.

The geese that flew over going south last week, flew back across going north yesterday. I *told* you that old gander was lost and wouldn't ask for directions! Did I also tell you that I saw a blue heron in our creek? What a thrill. I have seen lots of white herons, but this is the first time I've seen a blue one. I startled it, and it flew off, upstream. It was so beautiful, I just stood in awe. God sure did an awesome job in creating some beautiful creatures and scenery. His only 'goof' was creating man, and I'm sure He has regretted it ever since.

Our first Bible Study starts this Wednesday, and I've been looking forward to it for the past two months, so you know what that means. . . I'll probably forget to go! Right now, they don't have a study group leader, so I guess they are just 'winging it.' God will work it out. He always does.

A good, stiff breeze came up, plucking the first dead leaves off the trees, swirling them around in an amusement park ride before scattering them across he lawn like confetti in a New York, ticker-tape parade. The breeze will cool things off nicely for working in the yard this evening.

It is so pretty here. I wish you could see this place. Most of all, it is peaceful. No fire or police sirens going off all night, no gunshots, barking dogs, loud acid rock or rap garbage at all hours of the day and night. Whenever I start feeling stressed out, I go sit in the back yard and listen to the soft murmur of the stream, or the breeze sighing through these tall oaks and elms. At least, I think they are elms. Not sure what kind, but they have been here a long time.

Several times I've heard a bird calling from the creek, but I never could see it, and I'm not good at identifying bird calls. Wish I were. Anyway, while I was outside trying to spot it, I was treated to the sight of a beautiful woodpecker. He was pretty high up in the tree, so I couldn't get a good look at the front of him, but, I think it was a Pileated Woodpecker. He had black and white stripes on the side of his head, a bright scarlet head and black shiny feathers. He looked like he was dressed in his tuxedo, ready to go to the ball.

Must get this ready to mail. Sending my love and prayers, as ever,

Shirlene and Harry

October 1, 2000

Dear Friends and Family,

Our weather is now in the 'iffy' stage—can't make up its mind. The mornings are cool enough for a sweatshirt, and the afternoons are hot enough to change to a light-weight blouse. Harry had a light frost on his windshield one morning, but no damage to any plants. I did, however, bring in my potted orange and lemon trees. Next year, I hope to have a greenhouse for them, but for this year, I have the orange tree by a nice window in the sewing room, and the lemon tree by a window in the den.

The pleasant, lazy days of late summer-early fall are here. The *days* are lazy, certainly not either of us. Harry is frantically trying to get the kitchen ready for the soon-to-arrive cabinets, and I am running around like a chicken with its head cut off, trying to take care of last minute details. I've ordered the kitchen counter top and now must find and order wallpaper and carpet, amid trying to keep up with all the outside and inside work. Fortunately, I feel better than I have felt in years! I still have bad days, and yes, I have to be careful not to get carried away and over do it, but for the most part, I'm doing really well. Last week I gave myself a perm and a hair cut, which is a two-hour job with my arms over my head most of the time, and then, that evening, I mowed all of our yard. A bit too much for one day, and I paid for it the next two days. I never seem to learn, but it's hard not to do things when I am feeling good. I've never been able to sit still and do nothing. Anyway, I'm just praising God for every day.

We finally verified what has been stealing the cat food. Racoons! That didn't surprise me, from the footprints I had found. Harry has to be at work at 6:00 a.m., so he leaves when it is still dark. One morning on his way out, he heard the thieves running away, so the next morning he took a flashlight with him and shined it in the cat's feeding area. Two big, fat racoons scampered off the shelf and headed for the creek. Getting fat on my cat food!

Critters outside, critters inside! I told you about the big, black beetles I killed out by the garage. Well, with Harry taking out wall board he has removed and bringing in supplies, some of the outside critters have invited themselves inside. I was sitting here a few nights ago, and I looked up on the ceiling above my head. It was a b-I-I-I-g bug. At first glance, I thought it was one of those awful black beetles, but when I looked closer, I realized it was a verrrry big grasshopper. I'm not afraid of them, but I didn't especially want him dropping down into my hair, so I got the step stool and one of my tennis shoes, and hit him. Instead of dying like and self-respecting, smacked bug is supposed to do, he dropped down inside the floor lamp. He wasn't quite dead, so I got a can of bug spray and gave him a bath. I left him to float around in his own bug juice until morning when I could dump him and clean the lamp.

Tonight I glanced up, and there was a big, black spider on the ceiling. Not a black widow, I don't think, but an ugly spider, nonetheless. Stool, tennis shoe, smack! The exterminator strikes again. I'm beginning to feel like an attendant at The Ugly Bug Ball! Someone ought to tell these bugs that the inside of my house is death row. No escape, no mercy. Zap! The bug war has begun.

Well, things are progressing on the kitchen. "Demolition Harry" has everything torn out to the 2' x 4's, a hole cut in the ceiling and the skylight installed, but not complete on the inside, and plumbing pipes sticking up with caps on them. Cabinets are to arrive October 4th, and then the demolition process gets reversed. Hopefully.

Of course, I've been very helpful. Whenever Harry lifts something heavy, I stand behind him and grunt for him. Uhhhhh, umph! Uhhhhh, umph! I figure he can't lift and grunt at the same time, but I get the feeling he doesn't always appreciate my helpfulness. I keep telling him, *"You can't hardly* get this kind of help anymore!" He rolls his eyes toward the ceiling and mumbles something that sounds suspiciously like "thank goodness."

Harry said he was tired today at work and didn't think he could hold up through the day. I told him, "No problem with tomorrow, I starched your shorts!" I didn't really, but now he's afraid to wear the ones I just washed. He's not really too sure whether I did it or not. The only thing I promised him when we got married was that life with me would never be boring. He says I've kept that promise.

We probably will get our wood stove installed sometime in November, and I can't wait. I had a wood stove when I previously lived in Oregon, and I loved it. It's so much warmer than any other kind of heat. Somehow, backing up to a forced-air, heat register to warm your backside just doesn't get it! Besides, you can't keep a pot of water on the heat register for hot coffee, chocolate or tea.

They are trying to incorporate our little town, and most of us don't want it incorporated. But, there is a possibility if we don't incorporate, we may be annexed into Grants Pass which would result in higher taxes than incorporation, and leave us without much, if any, representation. Taxation without representation—another Boston Tea Party! We probably won't get as far as a revolution, but, we went to one of the incorporation meetings, and I thought some of the opposing sides were going to come to blows. Actually, it was rather entertaining. My personal view is that we should have taken a large piece of black plastic to spread on the floor to catch some of the fertilizer fallout! Spread thick and heavy. Uh-huh!

The cats are locked up, the dog is in her cozy shed, Harry has gone to bed (escaped, I think), and I probably should do the same. To borrow a line from *The Sound of Music,* "The sun has gone to bed, and so must I."

May God bless you with sweet peace,

Shirlene and Harry

October 5, 2000

Dear Friends and Family,

Harry has been crawling around under the house, rerouting the plumbing, and I warned him to beware of the Boogie Man. He said, "Uh-huh," as he went out, but I noticed he took a light with him when he crawled under. *Ev-very* one knows that the light scares away the Boogie Man! However, I don't think it has much affect on spiders and crawly things. When he came back out he said, "If you're ever under there. . ." I interrupted him, "Trust me on this one. I will *never* be under there!" I *gave* him that part of the house, totally, unchallenged, as his complete and never-to-be-trespassed-upon domain. He can rest assured that territory will never be violated by me!

We bought some of those electrical sound things that are supposed to get rid of gophers. HA! They've made enough new tunnels underneath our back lawn to hold grand ballroom dancing, and I suspect they're using our "electrical sound" as their rock and roll music! I can just see them, digging in time to the beep-beep. *Dig, dig, rock. Dig, dig, roll. Yeah, man, dig!* We've got twice the tunnels now that we had when we put those stupid things in the ground. I even resorted to some poisoned grain poured down a couple of gopher holes, but I think it had the combined effects of grow-pup and hormones! Maybe I could trap a few of them and send them out as Christmas gifts. Watch your mail!

I don't know if you remember the movie, *Paint Your Wagon*, which I believe came out in 1969. Some of the miners dug tunnels under the town and mined the gold dust that was falling through the cracks of the floor boards in the saloons. Finally, they had so many tunnels that the whole town sank down into them. Well, I suspect that is going to happen to our back yard. I'm going to be mowing the lawn, and the garden tractor and I will slowly sink down into the abyss of gopher tunnels, like the sinking of the *Titanic*, never to be seen again.

After this kitchen remodel is completed (if it ever is), I think I'll do a new cookbook called *Remodeling Recipes.* Should be a big hit with anyone who has ever gone through, or will in the future go through, a remodel. Or maybe I'll call it *How to Wash Dishes In The Laundry Room Washtub.* "How To" books seem to sell pretty well. Probably the best title would be *Survival!* I'll have to think about it, but the possibilities are endless.

I ordered the kitchen carpet today and, earlier this week, ordered some of the herb and wildflower tiles that will go in back of the range. I'm trying to decide about wallpaper, and the kitchen counter was ordered last week, so it is gradually all coming together. The kitchen cabinets arrived Tuesday evening, October 3rd instead of October 4th, and they are now safely in the garage with the other kazillion boxes of 'stuff.' Harry said, (very apologetically) "I'm afraid it's going to be another week before I'll be able to start installing."

"Don't worry about it," I told him, "It will get done when it gets done. We're not on a time schedule. Just do it at your own pace." (He puts a lot of pressure on himself.)

Actually, I think it will probably be a couple of weeks, yet, before he can start installing them. There is still much to be done, but we've made out this long, so what's a couple more weeks? For the amount of work that had—and still has—to be done on this kitchen, he has done wonders! No complaints from this peanut gallery.

Last night, Harry wanted to take a break from the kitchen remodeling, so he went outside and worked on the planter bed for my daffodils. Tonight, I planted 175 daffodils and have about 40 more to plant, but I ran out of room. I also have about 200 tulip bulbs to plant, but I'm not even going to think about that for a while. I think in the past few years I must have grown a couple of feet taller because I noticed when I have to plant something, the ground is a lot farther away than it used to be. And the older I get, the farther away it gets.

October 9, 2000

Several years ago, while I was in Victoria, British Columbia visiting, I bought some really good tea. It is the same tea that they serve at the Empress Hotel, and I have used it sparingly to make it last. However, all good things eventually run out, and so it was with my special tea. I called Murchie's, the shop in Victoria where I purchased the tea, and ordered two pounds of the Empress Blend. I'm having a cup of it now, so get your own cup of coffee or tea, find a comfortable chair, and we'll finish our visit.

We've been having cool nights and warm days in the seventies and eighties, but this morning I awoke to gray skies and fifty degree temperature. Before 9:00 a.m., it was raining. The woods are so dry, and there have been so many fires this year, I was hoping for a good drenching rain, but, it rained so softly I had to stand under the sky light to hear the light tippity, tip-tap. It's not as good as hearing rain on a tin roof, but it is pleasant, nonetheless. I've always liked the sound of rain, and I love the clean, fresh-washed air.

I can't stay in a stuffy house all day, so I waited until the rain turned to a light mist and then went outside to give Schatze some food and water and to check the creek to see if the rain in the mountains has had time to reach our area. Evidently not, or there was so little the effect was almost negligible, because the creek had only risen about a half inch. There is a partially submerged block of cement in the creek that had APR 1 and a child's hand print. It is on its side with the AP out of the water and the R partially submerged. I can usually determine how much the creek has risen by checking the lettering on the block. I have been thinking about getting a long pole, marking it every six inches and sticking it in the creek. It would be interesting to see how much the creek will rise this winter when we start having some real rain.

It is early afternoon now, and the sun is breaking through the light, cloud cover and hitting the raindrops on the long-needled pine outside the dining room window, making each drop sparkle like tiny, white lights on a Christmas tree.

Rainy days usually inspire me to cook, but, since I don't have a kitchen, I settled for giving the house a good cleaning. It's almost impossible to keep things clean and orderly with the remodeling going on, but this morning, I gave it the old 'college try.' I figure if I can keep some semblance of order among this remodeling *in*sanity, I may be able to maintain some level of sanity. So, I scrubbed and cleaned bathroom sinks, tile, mirrors and anything else that got in my way, polished living room coffee and end tables, gathered rain-sprinkled roses and did a flower arrangement for the living room, washed six loads of clothes and am taking a break before vacuuming. I also have to open mail, pay bills, write (business)

51

letters, and finish this letter and get it ready to mail. I'll be glad when the kitchen is completed. Baking cookies would have been easier!

Harry has been working hard to get all the plumbing and electrical wiring done before the weather gets really cold. The sky light he installed on the roof over the kitchen can't be finished on the inside until the electrical work is completed, and until it is finished, we can't turn on the heat because all the heat would go UP (heat rises!) through the open sky light into the attic. Fortunately, it hasn't been too cold up to this point. We've only had a few nippy mornings when I've had to put on a sweater, but it usually warms up by noon, so it hasn't been a problem.

A couple of nights ago, I was sitting in the living room and Harry was working in the kitchen. He said, "I'm going to the switch box and check out these kitchen plugs." He plugged a lamp into one of them and asked, "Can you see this light from where you are sitting?"

I looked through the open 2' x 4's into the kitchen. "Sure."

"Okay," he said. "Just yell at me."

As he started down the hall I yelled, **"HARRY, YOU ROTTEN, GOOD-FOR-NOTHING TURKEY! WHEN ARE YOU GOING TO QUIT GOOFING AROUND AND GET SOMETHING DONE AROUND HERE?!"**

He turned around with a stunned look on his face. I grinned at him. "Well, you told me to **yell** at you. How am I doing?"

He went down the hall laughing and shaking his head. "That wasn't *exactly* what I had in mind."

I always try to be helpful.

In the few days between the start of this letter and the finish, I managed to get 63 tulips planted. I'm putting a lot of them in planter boxes and tubs to keep them away from the gophers. Don't know how many more I have to plant, but I suppose it will get done somewhere along the way. The previous owners had a few rose bushes, but no other flowers, so with all the space I have for planting, I'm scattering flowers all over the place. I can hardly wait for everything to bloom in the spring.

I woke up wheezing, coughing and sneezing this morning, so I started the day with a cup of Stinging Nettle tea and soon was breathing easier and the wheezing stopped. When the kitchen is finished (*ev-ve-ry* thing seems to hinge on that darn kitchen!), I'm going to start cleaning out the toxins and get this allergy/asthma *cured* instead of just treating the symptoms. I did it thirty years ago (when the allergies were much worse than now) and wasn't bothered by allergies again for almost twenty years. For the last ten years, they have been building up again, so I guess it is time to take the cure. Not difficult or bad, it just takes time, and I will have to be consistent.

I want to thank those of you who are keeping touch, either by phone or by letter. A couple of people have written with apologies that they don't write "as well as I do." Dear Ones, please don't feel that way. One of the persons I hear from regularly is legally blind, and sometimes, the lines of her letters slant down the page, and it is difficult to make out some of the writing; but my heart rejoices each time I get a letter from her. *Her letters are among my dearest treasures.*

When I receive a letter from someone, I'm not looking for how well it is written. (My own are written hastily and have some problems.) What I see is an offering from a loved one or valued friend that says, "I care enough to make the effort to keep in touch." My father was dyslexic and only had a third-grade education, and his grammar and spelling weren't great. Yet, the few letters I received from him when I was living out of state, were worth more to me than gold. *Your* letters to me are valued because *you* are valued, because they are written with a caring heart and received with the same. They mean more to me than a letter written by a Nobel Peace prize-winning writer. Please know that whatever you write, however it is written, will be received with love and thankfulness.

Well, I've procrastinated long enough, so I'd better get out the vacuum and finish my cleaning. Will try to get this in the mail by tomorrow, and will keep you dear people in my prayers and thoughts until next visit.

Our love,

Shirlene and Harry

October 12, 2000

Dear Friends and Family,

This past week a friend of mine, and one of my relatives, passed away, and I feel sad about losing them. They both rejected Christ and went into eternity unsaved. I guess I feel sad and somewhat responsible for their lack of salvation because I was unable to reach them. I tried, but perhaps I just wasn't able to make clear enough the difference between 'religion and church' and 'salvation and a personal relationship with Christ.' They aren't the same thing.

Some people are religious about a baseball or football team, but it won't get them into Heaven. Many people worship pagan gods, i.e., Buddhism—Muhammadanism worships Allah, the Moon God—and some cultures still practice human sacrifice. That's just religion, but it won't give you eternal salvation.

The same thing is true about church. A very wise minister once told me, "No church can save you or get you into heaven. Only a personal relationship with Christ will do that." Not all people who attend church are Christians. Some go because it is expected, because it makes them feel better, because they are trying to impress someone—for many varied reasons—but many who attend have never accepted Christ as their savior and have no personal relationship with Him. Praise God, they are in church where they will at least hear the plan of salvation.

Some people try to work their way into heaven by doing good deeds, or being what the world considers "good" people. The Bible says *"None are good. No, not one. For all have sinned and fallen short of the glory of God."* Rom.3:23. And, we aren't saved by anything *we* do. Salvation is a gift, freely given, by a Savior who took our sin upon Himself and paid our penalty on the cross. Only He can offer salvation. It is a free gift, freely given, and the price has already been paid.

We are all going to spend eternity—ongoing, *never ending*—somewhere, either in Heaven or Hell, and it makes me sad when people deliberately choose to spend it in Hell. Christ said, *"He who isn't with me is against me,"* Matt.12:30, so anyone *not* choosing Christ and eternal salvation has made the choice for Hell and eternal damnation. It is **not** going to be a nice place, and there isn't going to be a second chance to change your mind.

When I think of the peace I have and the joy that has been in my life, even in the midst of the greatest problems and difficulties in my life, I want that same peace and joy for everyone I know. Yes, even my enemies! Whatever peace and joy we have here on this earth will be multiplied a thousand times hereafter, and so will the torment of Hell. I wouldn't wish anyone to spend an eternity in Hell, especially when Christ says we only have to ask, and He will answer.

Some of my friends and family are saved, and I rejoice in their salvation because I know when they, and I, pass from this world, we will someday be reunited again. But, I also know that some of my friends and family are not saved, have not asked Christ for forgiveness and accepted His gift of eternal life, and I feel a deep grief for those persons who may go into eternity without salvation.

Where are you, today? Do you have that personal relationship, peace and deep joy that only the Holy Spirit can bring? I hope so. In fact, I pray so. If you haven't already done so, please, *please* make a decision **now** to accept Christ. None of us have a guarantee that we will be here even one more day. Don't face eternity without Christ. Ask Him for salvation and forgiveness. He said, *"Ask, and it shall be given unto you."* Because I love you, and Jesus loves you, my heart is very heavy for those of you who may not be saved. Please don't put it off until it is too late. I'm praying for you.

In love,

Shirlene

October 20, 2000

Dear Friends and Family,

WALLS! I now have *walls* in my kitchen! After almost two months of looking through open 2' x 4's, it almost feels claustrophobic. Should be able to start installing cabinets within the next ten days or so. Hope to have the kitchen all finished before Thanksgiving. Guess what I'll be thankful for?

Someone asked me if Harry was an electrician, and commented how fortunate that he can do all these things. I agree. I told them, "No, he isn't an electrician. He can do electrical, plumbing and carpentry—but he can't sing!"

Did you read about the helicopter crews that were kidnapped in South America? Well, five of those people work for Erickson Air Crane, where Harry works. I'm praying for their safe release.

On Monday, I was backing my pickup under the RV carport where I park, and I stopped half-way under to check on something at the back. I placed the truck in park, put on the emergency brake and got out. I guess the gear wasn't firmly into park, and the motion of getting out jarred it back into reverse. The truck started going backward, and I jumped in and slammed on the brake, but not quite fast enough to prevent the door from catching on the corner post, which pushed it back and sprang both door hinges.

On Tuesday, I took it to an auto body shop, and they were going to fix it temporarily so I could open and close the door, until they could get to it today to repair it. Through a miscommunication between the owner and the employee regarding the temporary repair, the employee damaged the front fender near the door. (Never did figure out why?!) Murphy's Law is still well and operating! Anyway, today my truck is in the shop being repaired (or further destroyed).

On mornings when I don't have to run errands or be any particular place, and could sleep in, those are the mornings I am awake and up by 6:00 or 6:30 a.m. On mornings when I have to run errands and *must* be up early, *those* are the mornings I am in a nice, deep, peaceful sleep and could sleep until 8:00 or later! Such was this morning. I had a really peaceful night's sleep, was snuggled into the featherbed like a newborn chick under an old hen, and could have slept until at least 8:00, but, of course, the alarm went off at 6:00, and I had to get up to take the truck to the shop by 8:00. Murphy's Law, again.

The weather forecast was for clouds and zero chance of rain, but they should have checked with me before printing that in the paper. I certainly could have told them it was going to rain. I washed my pickup and gave it a thorough cleaning, and that is a sure-fire rainmaker. Sure enough, it rained all last night, and it will probably rain all of today. Forget the Indian Rain Dances. I've got a fail-proof method.

The man who drove me home from the body shop said, "We wash all the vehicles after we repair them."

"Well, you won't have to wash mine. I just washed it two days ago. Besides, it's raining."

"Doesn't matter. The boss wants it done, so rain, shine or snow, I'm outside washing vehicles."

Since he washes them *outside,* and it is pouring rain, when I go back, I'll ask him if he dried it. Seems silly to me to stand out in the rain and wash a vehicle.

When I open the garage door in the mornings to let the cats outside, they go dashing out to freedom. This morning when I opened it, they dashed out about two feet and got hit by the rain. They skidded to a stop, ran back into the garage and meowed at me like it was my fault they got wet. Since I caused the rain by washing the truck, I guess they are right.

For a brief respite, the sun is shooting through an open-ing in the clouds, hitting water puddles and blindingly reflecting back off them. The warmth of the sun is causing steam to rise off the wooden fences and roof tops, and the fresh-washed grass is a brilliant Crayola-colored green, accentuated against red geraniums. A few trees, wearing new rust and yellow leaves, are stuck randomly among the evergreens, decorating the hillsides like ornaments on a Christmas tree. God's handiwork!

They brought my pickup home a little after 6:00 p.m., and it looks great. After the man left, I pulled onto the grass area and tried to back into the RV area where I park. Ha! "Rot'sa Ruck!" The truck sank like the *Titanic*, down into the mud-that-was-grass, and wouldn't go forward or backward. Great! Stuck in the mud in my own back yard. Don't ask me what kind of week this has been.

I got out (in the rain) and opened a pack of roofing shingles we had stored at the back of the RV area, and wedged roofing shingles, tightly, under the back and front of the rear wheels, so I would have traction. Then, I slowly backed up on the back shingles, got out and moved shingles in front of the wheels and managed to pull forward onto the graveled drive. Boy, was my white truck a muddy mess! Since it was raining, I just hosed it down. I threw a few roofing shingles in the back of the truck, in case I get out someplace away from home and get stuck.

The fall after I graduated from high school, my dad and I went hunting in the mountains above Browns Valley. We got on a dirt, back road and parked to wait for daylight. It was raining, so Dad got in the back seat, I stayed in the front, and we took a nap. We were miles away from the main road and by the time the rain let up, the car was well mired into the mud. Dad got out and chopped off some evergreen branches, used a shovel to dig out in front and back of the wheels, wedged evergreen branches under the tires, and we pulled right out of that mud hole. My Dad was a pretty clever, resourceful guy, and I never forgot the lesson. Today, all those many years later, it came in handy. Thanks, Dad.

I've been intending to put gravel in the area in front of the RV parking, so I guess I'll have to stop procrastinating and get it done if I want to park under there this winter. I don't know why they made an RV parking area back there and then planted grass in the driveway. Not much common sense, considering Oregon's rain. When this ground gets wet, the mud is as slippery as a greased pig and as treacherous as quicksand. If it gets much wetter, I'll have to start carrying one of those little flags on a long pole. Then, if I sink out of sight in the mud, someone might spot the flag and know where to dig for me in the spring.

When I got my two cats, the woman said, "I can't tell you how many evenings I've spent calling, "Here, kitty, kitty," trying to catch all my cats and get them in for the evening so they will be safe."

I grinned. "I'm not about to chase cats. I'll train them to come in."

"Well, good luck!" she told me.

I rang a little dinner bell when I put their food out and had them trained in two days. Now, when I want them to come in for the night, I ring the dinner bell, and they come running. Mischief, a.k.a., Gluttonpuss, is usually inside the garage waiting, but C.C. (Compact Cat) is often out somewhere on the property, as she was tonight. I rang the dinner bell several times, and she came running from the pasture and skidded to a stop in front of the food dish. I figure I'm smarter than the average cat!

October 21, 2000

Harry has been sealing and sanding kitchen walls, which puts a layer of fine white dust over everything in the house. Trying to keep the house clean while he is working is a lost cause. The good news is, the walls are now primed and ready for paint. I special-ordered some tiles with herbs on them, for the back splash in back of the range, and they are all here, ready for installation. The carpet for the kitchen is ordered, although finding a carpet installer may be a problem, but each day sees some new thing being accomplished. It's sort of like being on a slow boat to China.

It occurred to me today that we are barely two months away from Christmas, so I worked on a few Christmas items and ordered a few more. With all we've got going, I probably won't be doing as much this year as in the past, but it really doesn't matter. It's all about honoring Christ anyway. Past that point, it is irrelevant.

The rain let up late this afternoon, and the sun peeked through a patchwork of gray and white clouds to spotlight dark blue mountains. My yard is once again blanketed with leaves, the blister from last week's raking hasn't yet healed. . . and there is still a ton of leaves on the trees just waiting for me to get the yard cleaned again. I reeeeallly don't want to think about it. Like Scarlet O'Hara, "I'll think about it tomorrow."

I'd better think about getting this ready to mail, so I'll leave you for now, but stay tuned for the next installment. (I wonder if I could get a sponsor for this Soap Opera?)

Our love and prayers,

Shirlene and Harry

October 24, 2000

D ear Friends and Family,

"*This is the day the Lord has made. I will re-joice and be glad in it!*" It has been said there are two kinds of people in the world. Those who wake up and say, "Good morning, Lord," and those who wake up and say, "Good Lord, it's morning!" I'm the first kind and Harry is the second, so we cover both bases. Harry complains every day about having to get up so early and go to work, but, on the weekend when he *could* sleep in, he gets up early, so he can wake me up! I think there's a streak of vindictiveness in there!

At 7:00 a.m., the temperature was thirty degrees and a fine layer of frost covered everything. It is now almost 9:00 a.m., and the temperature has climbed to a warm and cozy thirty-three degrees! Wish I had my new wood stove to cuddle up to, but that is at least a month away, possibly two months. Harry has about all the projects he can handle right now, trying to finish the kitchen. He's doing a great job, but it is really a lot of work. Wonder if I could 'clone' him? I'm sure he could use the help! On second thought, I'm not sure I could deal with two. . . scratch that 'clone!'

I'm supposed to go out today and get another half cord of firewood, but, at the moment, the neighbors' houses are playing hide-and-seek in the fog, so I've put the firewood on hold until this fog burns off. It's usually gone by afternoon. With fire season officially over, we can now burn our brush piles. Maybe, if I go light the brush piles, it will burn off the fog.

The fog burned off around 10:30 a.m., and the sun blazed in all its brilliance. I don't know what the temperature was, but, by the time I got the truck loaded with wood, I was *pu-lenty* warm! That should be the last time I have to do this. We now have over a cord of seasoned oak, and that should take us through the winter. Hopefully, by next year, we'll have wood from the trees we have to cut down here, on our property.

Harry got off work early today and I told him, "Gee, honey, I'm so glad you came home early. I have this really fun thing for you to do." I don't know why he looks at me so suspiciously when I tell him things like that.

"What?" I don't think he ree-alll-ly wanted to know, but I told him anyway. "I got another load of wood, and it needs to be unloaded and stacked. Won't that be *fun?*" He went off mumbling, "Uh-huh, yeah!" I got the feeling I really didn't convince him how much fun he was going to have, but he'll thank me later this winter when we have a nice, cozy fire.

October 26, 2000

I gave Harry fair warning some time ago that if we moved onto acreage, I was going to have a large guard dog. It's not that I want a dog that will run out and bite someone, but larger dogs are more intimidating. Schatze, all fifteen pounds of her, runs at anyone who comes on the property and proceeds to attack by jumping up and licking them to death. I admit the jumping and licking isn't very pleasant, but I don't think it would tend to discourage a trespasser.

For those of you (including Harry) who have occasionally questioned my sanity, I probably should admit you are at least *partially* correct. A guy in the parking lot at the bank had a box full of six-week-old puppies, and I picked one out.

"Is that one a female?"

He said, "Yes." He lied, but I trusted him, so, without checking, I brought the puppy home. Only then, did I discover it was a male. Admittedly, a puppy isn't exactly what I needed in the middle of all this remodeling. Right now, he is cute and cuddly, but, if his feet are any indication, when he is grown I can probably buy a saddle and ride him. I named him Duke.

October 30, 2000

I made a bed for Duke in a large dog carrier, put him in my bedroom and was up with him every two hours the first couple of nights. Last night was the first decent sleep I have had since Duke joined our family, but I think he is over his fright and settling in. Schatze terrorizes him, and the cats have boxed his ears a couple of times, but he is gradually finding his place among the menagerie.

I've taken Duke in the pickup a couple of times, and he doesn't get sick. **HALLELUJAH**!! The first eight months after I got Schatze, every time I put her in the truck she would look around, figure out that she was in a moving vehicle (even if it wasn't moving), and bla-uuph, all over the towels and newspapers I had used to upholster the inside of the truck. Duke looks around, curls up on the seat and goes to sleep. I like it!

The weather forecast says it will freeze tonight, and I don't doubt it. When I took Duke out around 6:30 this evening, the air was crisp and cold, and I could see my breath. The clouds from the past couple of days of rain had disappeared, and I could see stars sparkling like tiny diamonds scattered across a black velvet sky.

Our creek came up several inches during the last rains. It's funny how it changes its expression with the change in the weather, reflecting back the face of the sky. On sunny days the creek is clear and cheerful as the bright blue sky, but, on gray days, it reflects back the grayness with a darkness that makes the rushing water appear cold and threatening. With the rise in the water level, it is also running faster, and I can hear its hasty progress clear across the yard.

I read a statistic the other day that said large trees—the kind we have—have over 100,000 leaves on them. We have approximately twenty large trees in the back, so I'll let you do the math on the number of leaves covering the yard, waiting to be raked. Waaah! (Don't you hate to see a grown woman cry?)

We're running into the usual amount of problems and delays with the cabinets, but I won't get into that tonight. It's late, so I'll take Duke out one more time, and go to bed. G'night.

October 31, 2000

We now have the upper cabinets installed on the left (south) side of the kitchen, a pantry sitting temporarily at the end, and the oven cabinet with the oven sitting in it, not yet wired for use, but looking pretty impressive. I can't cook anything in it, yet, but I can make mud pies and pretend. Guess what Harry gets for dinner?

I knew that living on this piece of property back off the road would have its advantages. Tonight is Halloween, and I only had one trick-or-treater—and that was Harry! He thought the disguise would fool me, but I recognized him immediately when he pulled a toy gun and demanded to know where I had hidden the chocolate chips.

God keep you until next visit. Our love and prayers,

Shirlene and Harry

November 18, 2000

D ear Friends and Family,

The cabinets and oven are installed. Progress! Now we get to play "hurry up and wait." The counter top has been ordered, and, **if** it arrives on time, they will come back and install it November 28th. *Then*, Harry has to install the range top, sink, garbage disposal and dishwasher. *Then*, we have at least another week to get the carpet installed. I figure four or five more weeks, hopefully completed before Christmas. ("Hello, Denny's? We'd like to make a reservation for Thanksgiving.") Maybe I'll just run away from home and come back next year when everything gets back to normal. At this point, I'm not really sure what 'normal' is!

It really *is* beginning to resemble a kitchen. The cabinets are a warm, honey-spice oak and, when it's all finished, I'm sure it will be pretty; but four-and-one-half to five months without a kitchen is a long wait. If this is supposed to teach me patience, I don't think it is working.

We've had some very whimsical weather, but I think that is not unusual for this time of year. We have a couple of days of misty rain, a few days of fog, and a day or two of frost. Then, brilliant sunshine lures us into a false sense of security before more cold weather dumps on us. Jack Frost is probably sitting in the top of one of these big denuded trees saying, "Nanner, nanner, nanner! Gotcha!"

Speaking of denuded trees, last weekend I hired a young boy to help rake and move all the leaves off the yard. The two of us worked over three-and-one-half hours—an equivalent of seven hours of raking—and still only got about two-thirds of it done. Now, the trees are finally bare of leaves with only the green moss covering the limbs, like an old man in grimy long johns.

Actually, we haven't had much rain, just a lot of Oregon mist. (I think it "missed" Washington, and hit Oregon.) I look outside and can't see any rain, but everything is wet. Then, I go out and a find a fine mist falling. I think it is what the weather people like to call "precipitation." In translation, that means "It gonna' rain on yo' haid!"

The mist soaks the long needles on the pine trees, then slowly drips off the ends of the needles. When the sun hits it, all the tiny drops of water on the ends of the needles look like small, twinkling lights on a Christmas tree.

All of our animals are eating a lot and putting on weight, which is a sign of a long, cold winter. I'm trying to convince Harry that's what I'm doing, storing up for a long, cold winter; but, he gives me that "yeah, right!" look and somehow, I don't think he's buying it.

Funny how our sunrises have changed now that winter is here and the sun is rising lower on the southern horizon. Now, instead of bursting over the highest mountain in brilliant yellow, it sleepily crawls over the lower ridges in cold, white silver.

Postage rates are going up. . . again. You'd think with all the letters I write (approximately 48, once or twice a month) that the post office would be sufficiently supported. I'm certainly doing my part to support them! I tried to petition them for a discount, or perhaps a special non-profit rate (I'm certainly *not* making a profit!), but they wouldn't go for it. Very uncooperative.

Since I won't be able to cook on Thanksgiving, we are going to get away and visit Shore Acres State Park on the coast, near Coos Bay. They decorate the whole park in Christmas lights. There are supposed to be 225,000 lights this year, and they increase it every year. It should be interesting to see, but, mostly, it will be good to get away for a day or two.

When I told Harry what I wanted to do for Thanksgiving, he gave me a hug, laughed and said, "I think that's a great idea—as long as you're paying for it."

I came right back at him. "Honey, of course I'm paying for it—out of your paycheck."

He went down the hall, laughing. "That's what I figured."

As Thanksgiving approaches, I realize how many things I have to be thankful for, and I begin to count my blessings; a roof over my head when many are homeless, food on the table when millions are hungry, clothes to keep me warm, and a good bed for a comfortable night's sleep. The list could go on indefinitely. However, I realize the most important blessing is a Savior who died for a sinner like me (and you) that we might have eternal life, just by accepting Jesus. I don't understand the greatness of God's love for me, the depth that would allow him to send His only Son to die for *my* sins—I certainly couldn't give up a child or grandchild to save someone—but God did that for us. That is a love that is unfathomable. I may not be able to understand it, but I will be eternally grateful for the gift. And that is exactly what it is—a gift! Not something we can earn by being "good," but something freely given. That's grace, my friend. Amazing grace!

As my days on this earth are drawing nearer the end, I find myself praying more diligently than ever for those who are lost. I don't know where you are in relation to God and eternity, but I pray if you have not made the decision to turn your life over to Christ, you will do so. Christ said, *"I am the way, the truth and the life. No man (one) comes to the Father, except by me." (John 14:6.)* Think about it.

Have a wonderful Thanksgiving! Praying for you, as always,

Shirlene and Harry

November 21, 2000

Dear Friends and Family,

When my daughter was little and we had fog, she would say, "Mommy, it's froggy." Usually our fog lifts by noon, and we get sunshine; however, today has been one of those cold, "froggy" days where the fog doesn't go away.

It never got up to forty degrees today—just got enough above freezing to melt the ice in the dog's and cat's water dishes. I went outside for a short time to let Schatze out of the pen so the dogs could get some exercise, and to feed the birds. When I came back in, my hands were pretty cold, so I warmed them up on Harry. I keep reminding him he promised to love, honor and warm my cold hands and feet. He says he doesn't remember that, but I tell him it was in the fine print. If that doesn't work, I tell him he's too senile to remember.

It must be a couple of degrees warmer here than in Grants Pass and Medford. A few days ago, when I left Merlin to go shopping in Medford, the sun was shining here. The fog had not lifted from Grants Pass to Medford and the previous night's frozen frost was still on the trees. Outside branches of pine trees were sprinkled with frosty-white glitter, and bare trees held out branches clothed in "Winter's" finery. Tiny droplets of frozen fog drifted down, creating a micro-mini snow that covered plants, weeds, lawns and plowed fields in a dusting of powdered-sugar white. It was trying to snow, but never quite got up the nerve to do so. By the time I finished shopping and returned home, the sun was out and the magic had melted.

One morning recently, I was sitting in the living room, writing on the lap-top, and I glanced out the window. Tiny bits of white drifted down. Snow? I went to the porch to check. Yes! Snow. Gradually, it increased to big, fluffy flakes, but they were slushy and melted as soon as they hit the ground. That's okay, because I'm not much into shoveling snow. It was really beautiful to watch, though, and I enjoyed it for about an hour. Then it was gone.

Occasionally we have a clear, cold night that encloses the mountains in a black blanket and fringes it with stars. Even on most clear days, the clouds drop down around some of the mountains like a feather boa around a woman's shoulders. It is truly beautiful here, whatever the weather is doing.

November 28, 2000

We had plans to go to Shore Acres Park on Thanksgiving day, but we had fog and rain and weren't sure about going. We went out for dinner, came home and sat around for a while. The rain stopped, and the fog lifted from ground to high fog.

"Well, what do you think?" I asked Harry. "Should we go for it?"

Harry said, "Yeah, let's take a chance."

We quickly threw some things in the pickup and took off for Coos Bay. We prayed about it, of course, and asked for either clear weather or high fog so we wouldn't have any driving problems, and for good weather when we got there. We had high fog and good visibility all the way except for about two miles of low fog at the summit, but even that wasn't all that bad. About half way to Coos Bay, it rained on us, and we figured it might be raining when we got there. If so, we would be miserable, walking around and getting wet.

Just as we pulled into Coos Bay, the rain stopped. We checked into our motel and headed for the Park. The roads were wet, but no rain. We toured the park, saw all 225,000 lights, ate cookies and drank hot cider. As we were driving out of the park, it started raining again. The timing couldn't have been more perfect. The next morning as we left to come home, the sun was out at the coast, but about ten miles inland, we lost the sunshine and had very high fog, clouds with no rain and good driving conditions. God was with us all the way, and it really was a nice trip.

Kitchen update! Harry has the range hood installed, and the dishwasher is in although it can't be used until the counter top and sink are installed. I wish you could see the beautiful job Harry did on the installation of the cabinets. The man who measured for the counter top said the cabinets were more professionally done than by "professional" installers. He said, "You just don't see that quality of workmanship anymore." I agree.

The counter top was supposed to be installed today. When Harry came home and looked in the kitchen, he commented, "Oh, they didn't make it?"

I laughed. "You still believe in Fairy Tales? Just because they said they'd be here doesn't necessarily mean they will." Hopefully, maybe tomorrow.

Harry asked what I wanted for Christmas, and I told him, "I want the gate installed across the driveway. Then, I can let Schatze run free. That will be my (and Schatze's) Christmas present." He agreed. Harry hates to shop, so the gate installation solves his shopping problem.

When I let Schatze out of the pen, she goes up to the meadow and challenges the Greyhound on the other side of the fence to a race. His name is King and he is about ten years old. They race from one end of the fence to the other, then turn around and race back again. I don't know which dog enjoys it more. Schatze thinks she is in dog heaven, and King seems to be having a lot of fun, too. The exercise is good for both of them.

Duke has gained weight at about a half pound a day. At two-and-one-half-months old, he is now as big as Schatze. Although he is her size, he is slow and puppy-awkward, and she is as fast as greased lightening. She pounces on him, rolls him over and runs circles around him. With his big feet and clutzy-puppy ways, he doesn't stand a chance. When I put Schatze back in the pen, Duke comes running across the lawn to me, big ears flapping in the breeze. I think if he ever got control of them, he could fly. A doggy Dumbo!

He has been a pretty good puppy, other than pulling up my expensive Irises. He meanders over to the Iris bed, sniffs around to be sure he makes the right selection, grabs the top part of the most expensive bulb in his mouth and yanks. Wow, Mom! Look at the fun game I've invented! Then, he chews the heck out of the bulb. In defense of my bed of Irises, I bought chicken wire, and Harry built a fence around the Iris bed. The next morning Duke had a puzzled look on his face as he circled the Iris bed like a plane looking for a place to land. He figured there had to be some way to get in there. I think I spoiled all his fun.

Since Duke is getting so big, and I can no longer carry him around, I decided I should teach him to "heel" so I can put him on a lead when I take him to the vet. Duke had other ideas. The first two or three nights, I brought him into the house and walked him up and down the den area. He didn't do too badly. He figured it was some fun game we were playing, and, since it got him into the house, he went along with it. "Sit" was really easy. Plop! and he was down. Being naive, I figured it was time to take the training outside. Disaster! Once outside, Duke wanted to chase the cats, investigate leaves blowing around, check out the flower beds, and just generally run free.

We started with a cloth lead, which Duke took into his mouth and proceeded to demolish. Not to be outdone, I changed to a chain lead. No problem. He grabbed the chain in his mouth, then rolled over on his back with all four feet up in the air. Did you ever try to walk a dog that was in that position? After numerous attempts, we have finally advanced to partial cooperation. There is hope that he may yet get me trained.

Mischief and Duke have become pretty good buddies, and I often find them snuggled up together. Mischief eats Duke's dog food, and he reciprocates by eating the cat food. C.C. (Compact Cat) avoids them. She doesn't want any part of that dumb puppy.

I watched Mischief try to catch a bird today. She crept up to the base of the tree, climbed just to the bottom of the bird feeder, waited for a second, then swiftly shot up even with the feeder and grabbed for the bird. The bird flew away unharmed. Figuring she'd have a better chance, Mischief climbed *into* the bird feeder, which is just big enough to hold her, and sat waiting for a bird to fly into her mouth. **DUH!** I think the birds are pretty safe.

When we moved into this house, Harry figured we needed a 5-HP rototiller. The new ones run from around $560 - $900. **Not!** We looked in the paper, but the used ones were $200 - $300, and they were a piece of junk. I prayed about it, and we kept looking. Meanwhile, I forgot about the prayer.

Last night, Harry came home and said he saw a new 5-HP rototiller at Supply One (our local hardware/lumber store that is going out of business), and it was on sale for 30% off. The original price was $554. At 30% off, that left $388. Still a little pricy for our budget, however, Harry really wanted that rototiller. He called the manager and asked if he would sell it to us for 40% off. No, he had to sell it for the *marked* price. Yesterday was the last day of their liquidation sale, this was the last rototiller they had, and they were only going to be open for another thirty minutes. Harry thought it was still a good buy, so we jumped into the pickup and raced to the store to look at it.

When we arrived at the store, the manager Harry had spoken to was up front. Harry identified himself, and the manager said, "Oh, that rototiller you called about? I can't sell it to you for 30% off. I just checked the price in the computer, and it is marked at 50% off. Heck! If I'd known it was that good a price, I'd have bought it myself!"

Instantly, I remembered my prayer that God would help us find a good rototiller at a reasonable price, within our budget. When God answers, he doesn't fool around. We got a *new* rototiller for $277 dollars. God never ceases to amaze me! With that positive thought, I leave you with my love and prayers,

Shirlene and Harry

December 15, 2000

Dear Friends and Family,

    Since this will probably be the last letter I manage to write *this* year, I'll try to bring you up to date on the *Perils of Pauline,* a.k.a., the Perils of Shirlene! I haven't exactly been tied to a railroad track, but there have been days when I've felt as though the train had run over me. Some days, I feel totally fragmented!

    The kitchen is not yet finished, but it is functional, meaning it is usable. We still have things to complete; knobs on the cabinets, trim at the top, ceiling molding, five pull-out drawers to be built that were not included in the original order, window sill and frame to be finished, electrical outlet covers to be installed, one more corner cabinet to be hung, two corner shelves to be built and installed, and two under-cabinet shelves to be stained and installed. The good news is, all appliances, counter tops, sink and carpet are in. It actually *looks* like a kitchen. The bad news is, now Harry expects me to cook. What? And mess up my new kitchen?!

    We haven't had much rain here, one or two days, but today it is raining. It started out rather ho-hum, but it has gradually gotten serious. It was below freezing last night, but with today's rain, has warmed up to a toasty forty degrees. They are warning of some really cold weather this week and possible power outages. Wish we had our wood stove installed, but that probably won't happen for a couple more weeks.

    Duke is now three months old, weighs over twenty pounds and is an adorable klutz. He has a nice, cozy bed that the cats confiscate every day. He winds up on an old blanket on the porch, *outside* of his doghouse. It hasn't yet occurred to him that he is bigger than they are. I put some 'people' food in his dog dish, and both cats dived in before he could get to it. He plopped down on his rump and looked at me like, *Aw, Mom, look what they did!"* I said, "You're on your own, Buddy." He stood up, cocked his head to one side, then gave his mightiest "WOOF!" and both cats scattered. He's learning.

Harry got an unexpected Christmas bonus. Erickson is shutting down their entire operation from December 22nd to January 2nd, so all employees get a week off with pay. Nice Christmas present. Harry said, "Make a list of what needs to be done that week." Boy, DID I MAKE A *LIST*! I'll bet he'll be glad to go back to work when the ten days are over. He'll have to go back to work to rest up!

It seems that most of the Christmas Cards I have received are wishing me peace and joy, and it started me wondering how many people really have true peace and joy.

When Christ was born, an angel appeared to the shepherds, *And the angel said unto them, Fear not: for behold, I bring you good tidings of great **joy**, which shall be to all people. For unto you is born **this day** in the City of David, a savior which is Christ the Lord. (Luke 2:10-11.) And suddenly there was with the angel a multitude of the heavenly host praising God, and saying, Glory to God in the highest, and on earth **peace**, good will toward men. (Luke 2:13-14.) (emphasis mine.)*

I've read those verses many times, but only recently did the message take on new meaning. ***This*** day! Not hundreds of years ago, but the day you receive and acknowledge Christ as Savior. That is the day He will be born *unto you!* And from that day, you will have ***peace*** that passes understanding, and ***joy*** that flows like a river! Not because you will no longer have problems—you will. But peace and joy will flow *in spite of* your problems, so. . .

I wish you joy this Christmas Morn,

For unto you a child is born.

Angels wished the Shepherds peace on earth,

To celebrate this lowly birth.

They did not know what joy He'd bring,

Or understand He'd be a king.

He lived, He died, He came, He went,

And few realized He was Heaven sent.

The world goes on in its uncaring way,

But He still holds joy and peace, today.

My Savior died, salvation to bring,

When He comes back, He'll be a king.

He's bringing joy and peace unknown

For those He claims to be His own.

You can have that joy and peace, right now,

But only Christ can show you how.

So at this Christmas, embrace His love,

Accept His gifts from Heaven above.

For they will keep you all year through,

In His great love, so pure and true.

I wish you Christmas in your heart,

And may its wonders never depart.

May you always have His wondrous joy,

And the peace that came from this baby boy.

EIM

We send our sincere wishes for a Happy Christmas and a safe and happy New Year. May the joy of this season abide in you forever, and may you know God's everlasting peace and joy.

Shirlene and Harry

December 22, 2000

Dear Friends and Family,

Three days to count-down! No matter how much I think I am ready, I really never am. Christmas has the same effect as getting old—it gets here so *fast!*

I got the house decorated last week, and it is a good thing I did, because I sure wouldn't feel like doing it now. Harry gave me his cold, and he thinks that counts as a Christmas present, but he's not going to get away with that! I told him I'm going to do something really nasty to get even. He wanted to know "what?" so I sent him out in the mad rush of last-minute Christmas shoppers to run errands for me. That'll fix him!

When I told Harry I wanted the gate installed across the driveway for my Christmas present, I asked him, "How long do you think it will take Schatze to figure a way out, around or through that gate?"

I don't know what it is about Terriers, but they love to wander and they are excellent escape artists. Schatze is no exception to that rule. Every time we plug up an escape route, Schatze finds another one. She should have been named Houdini. Duke is really good about staying in the yard and hasn't shown any attempts to wander, but yesterday, I happened to go out to the garage and glanced in the direction of the highway. Schatze had found another exit and was out of her pen, marching down the lane to adventure, and was taking Duke with her. My 'cold' and I went out in the rain, got her back in her pen and nailed a board over her latest escape route. If I'd gotten Duke at the same time I got Schatze, I probably would have named them Adam and Eve, because she is always leading him astray!

Harry bought me a book, *The Mark*, for Christmas, brought it in and gave it to me, (unwrapped) and immediately sat down and started reading it.

I said, "You bought that for *whom?*"

A few days later, he brought me a bag of chocolate-covered orange sticks. When I thanked him for them, he said, "Don't think you're going to get all of those."

"You bought those for *whom?*"

I just took a pan of cornbread out of the oven, for my cornbread dressing, and I had a nice, big piece of it. Give me *old fashioned* (no sugar) buttermilk cornbread, and you can have all the cakes and cookies. Tomorrow night I'll stuff the turkey and will cook it Sunday. We'll have our big dinner

Christmas Eve day, attend the candlelight service at church, and have warm-ups on Christmas day, so I don't have to spend the whole day working in the kitchen. I got my pies cooked yesterday and put one in the freezer. Harry has already started on the other one, and he took a piece in his lunch. He asked why the pumpkin pie was brown. I told him it was full of Ex-lax. Do you suppose I should have told him it was the cinnamon? Naaah! That would spoil all the fun.

I sent my laptop to have a new "A" drive installed, and I really do miss it. Going from the laptop to my big, desk computer is like going from a jet plane to a Greyhound bus. Don't know how long they will have it, but it took them twenty days just to get the box to me for shipping, so if that is any indication, I may not have it back before next summer. Service, it ain't.

December 26, 2000

Ho, Ho, Ho! It's over for another year. I try to keep the Spirit of Christmas all year long, but I can do without the commercialism, thank you. It gets worse every year. I must have been dreaming when I thought I was going to make it to church on Sunday. My cold got worse, and I really was 'out of it' for a few days. I managed to get the dinner completed, a little bit at a time, but I didn't stick my nose out of the house for days except to take care of the animals. Fortunately, on Christmas day, my cold was better, and the sun was shining for most of the day. I managed to get outside for an hour or so. What a nice change.

Today started a bit cold, but the fog burned off, the sun came out, and I have been out several times, wandering in the fresh air with the dogs. Any day it isn't raining, I try to get outside for a while. I hate being stuck in a stuffy house. I don't think it is good for your health. When Harry gets the security doors installed, I can open the wood doors and air out the house. I probably freeze Harry half to death most of the time because I am always turning down the heat and opening the doors and windows. He's always complaining about being cold, so I bought him some heavy, quilted-flannel shirts for Christmas. If that doesn't work, I'm going to get him a Buffalo robe—with the Buffalo still in it!

I brought Schatze in on Christmas day to bathe her and discovered sores on her back where the ticks have been eating on her. Poor baby! I doctored her sores and declared that she is, hereafter, a house dog. Poor little mutt thinks she's died and gone to heaven. *You-know-who* isn't very happy about that decision, but he'll just have to live with it because I'm not going to put her back in that tick-infested pen. Schatze is awfully good in the house. She isn't a barking, yapping dog, she isn't the least bit destructive, she doesn't get on the furniture, and I can put her on her blanket and tell her to "stay," and she stays.

Duke is getting bigger every day. He is a well-marked, good-looking dog, with a marshmallow disposition. He must get that from his Golden Retriever mother. His coloring and markings look a lot like a Rottweiler with maybe a little Rhodesian Ridgeback thrown in, because he has a strip of hair down the center of his back that grows in a forward direction. It gives him somewhat of a fierce look, if you don't look at his soft eyes and puppy-grin. Personally, I like the combination—a sweet, loving disposition, with a fierce, intimidating appearance. I don't want a dog that will bite, just one that makes strangers wonder if he might. Actually, he is very shy and one of the most loving dogs I have ever owned. I think my fifteen pound "terror" would be more likely to bite someone, than Duke.

Airborne Express delivered my laptop today! Yea! Yea! Hooray!! I take back every nasty thing I was thinking about the computer company. Talk about answered prayer! I was absolutely thrilled to get it back. (Could you have guessed?) I had to delete things off the C drive when I sent it in for repair, and since the A drive wasn't working, I couldn't transfer to a floppy disc to save them, so I have quite a bit of re-typing to do. Harry thinks it will keep me out of mischief, but I doubt it.

We had several days of rain this past week and now Harry is out trying to burn water-soaked Evergreen branches. He has so much smoke out there I expected to see him doing an Indian war dance. He's certainly sending up enough smoke signals. I told him the only thing he is accomplishing is messing up the atmosphere. (The branches burned, but with LOTS of smoke!)

Thursday, December 28, 2000

Well, it has taken me almost a week to get this written, and I won't get it in the mail until tomorrow, so, by the time you get this, we will have another new year.

Harry now has the gate installed, but still has to install the automatic gate opener. Schatze has already been out examining it, looking for a way out. Annnnd, we have a new mailbox, thanks to a Christmas gift from my daughter and son-in-law. *Thanks, Kelly & Derek!*

The knobs and handles are on the kitchen cabinets, and the trim is finished. Harry has the five pull-out drawers made (that weren't sent with the order), but it will be a few days before they will be installed. A little here, a little there, and the kitchen is almost finished. It really looks nice. Just a few more things to finish. It has been a long haul!

I should be given a medal. I took both dogs to the Vet today—together—at the same time! Both are good when they are in the pickup, riding, but getting them in and out is a three ring circus. Duke is three months old now and getting too big to lift, so I place his front feet on the floor board of the back seat and proceed to lift his rear end while shoving forward, at the same time he is backpedaling! When I get him crammed into the back floor area, we go through much the same process to get him from the floor to the backseat. Once there, he lies down and goes to sleep. I don't wonder that *he* is exhausted. . . I sure am! Schatze is no big problem. I just pick her up and toss her on the front seat. However, once she is in and I am in, she backs up to me and keeps trying to work her way in back of me, between me and the seat. I keep pushing her across the seat, yelling, "Get over!" She has never liked riding in a motor vehicle.

When we arrive at the Vet's, I put Schatze on the ground and put my foot on her leash. This leaves me with both hands free to pull Duke out of the pickup, a process he fights with all his strength. Finally, pulling, tugging, dragging and lifting, I get him out, and we proceed into the office with Schatze straining forward on her lead (she likes the Vet's treats) and Duke sitting on his haunches, leaning back and dragging his feet like a car with the brakes locked. Anyone brave enough or crazy enough to take both these dogs to the Vet at the same time, deserves a medal for bravery and service above and beyond the call of duty!

Harry got a mechanical dog for Christmas. It is a battery operated Poo-Chi. Poo-Chi blinks its eyes, barks out six songs, dances on its toes and even snores when it is getting ready to go to sleep. (If I could set it to snore all night, I'd put it under

Harry's bed!) You don't have to feed or water it, no poop to clean up, and no trips to the Vet. Harry's kind of pet.

Schatze likes squeaker toys, and this mechanical dog is driving her crazy. Her tail is up and quivering, and she is at full attention. Wonder if it will get that kind of reaction out of Harry? If it does, it will be worth whatever it cost!!

I'd better get this ready to mail, so I'll close, sending our love, our prayers, and our Wishes for a Safe and Happy 2001

Shirlene & Harry

Part Two

2001

Dear Friends . . .

Judy Henry (Janelle's daughter) and Janelle Heatley
(Shirlene & Janelle have been friends since 1987)

Bill and Ann Davis, 2002
on their 47th Wedding Anniversary
Friends since 1955

Barb & Mary Gehr, 2001
Friends since 1960

Carol & Craig Hankins, Aug. 10, 2002
Carol and Shirlene share the same March 18th birthday
Friends since 1996

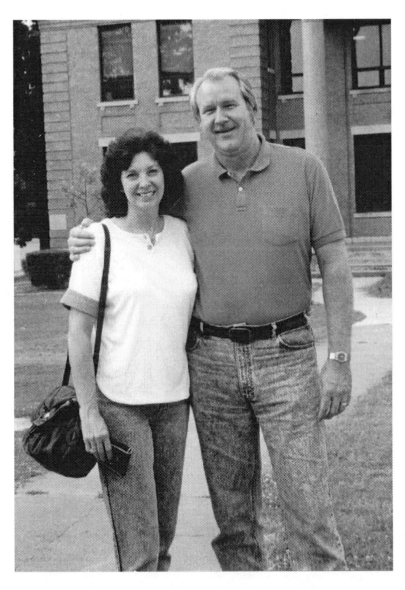

Shirley and Jim Brooks, 1991, Heber Springs, Arkansas
Friends since 1959

Robin and Wynn Lohner with Shirlene, 1988
Shirlene has been "2nd Mom" to Wynn since 1979,
and to Robin since 1988

Lt. Col. Tony DeJesus, Dec. 2003
Shirlene has been "2nd Mom" to Tony since 1985

Donna and Nellie Dennison
Friends since 1979

Ed and Joyce McColgan
Friends since 1991

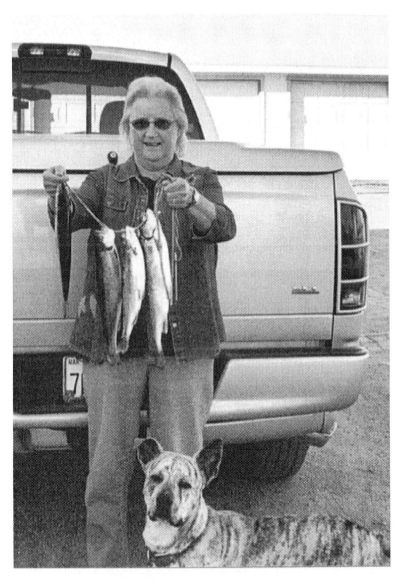

Shirley Easler and her dog, Grimmy
Friends since 1998

Inga and Bill Wynn
(Aunt and Uncle of Ed and Joyce McColgan)
in the Badlands of North Dakota, June 2002
Friends since 1992

Alberta Smith, Dec. 2005
Friend since 1992

Joyce Shults
Friend since 1998

Doug and Terri Wiley, Grants Pass, Oregon
Friends since February 2002

Nancy Saunders
Friend since 1998

January 1, 2001

D ear Friends and Family,

We ended the year yesterday with sunshine and sixty-three degree weather. Nice way to start the new year. Don't you love starting off a brand new year with a clean slate, no foul-ups or disasters. . . yet? Wouldn't it be nice to keep it that way all year? That's dreaming, of course, and it would probably be pretty boring.

I've heard that whatever you are doing on the New Year's day, you will be doing all year long. If that's true, Harry and I will be working as usual. He has been finishing up the kitchen pull-out drawers and putting up one of the kitchen shelves. I have been packing away Christmas decorations and trying to clean up the mess—polishing furniture, unpacking and washing crystal, doing laundry, taking care of the animals, and cleaning mirrors and glass doors on the china hutches. I think the last one was a waste of time because we are having the wood stove installed on Thursday, and I have a feeling I'll have to do the mirrors, glass and furniture again. With the kitchen almost completed, I have been able to unpack about ten more boxes. I am beginning to feel like we may, yet, get moved in and settled. But, now it's time to take a break and get the new year off to a grand start with a letter.

I've taken Schatze out several times today to play with Duke, and I get some exercise in the process because I have to stay out with them to watch Schatze. After Harry installed the gate across the drive, I put Schatze (a.k.a. Houdini) out the next day, and she went up into the pasture and found a way through the fence to visit my neighbor, Jo. Now, we have to get chicken wire to enclose the lower part of the fence in the pasture, so she can't get through. I think she considers it a challenge. *Now, where can I find my next escape route, and how long will it take me to find it?*

Duke is now three-and-one-half months old (four months on the 13th), weighs about 35-40 pounds, and the top of his back is about even with my knee. He is all legs, feet and floppy ears, and about as graceful as an elephant trying to put on panty hose. He chases Schatze but can never catch her, so he flops on the grass and rolls over, and she comes charging back and pounces on him. When he stands up, she walks under his belly and grabs his back leg. He has found the only way he can get the best of her is to grab hold of her collar. Then, she can't do anything. It's fun to watch them roll and run and play.

After being home for ten days, Harry goes back to work tomorrow (Tuesday, 2nd). TEN VERSES OF THE HALLELUJAH CHORUS!! I enjoyed the holidays, but I'm glad they are over, and we can get back to normal—whatever *that* is. My Christmas cold is in the last stages (I hope), and I'm ready to take on the world again. Already I've found out I'm on 'overloaded' for this year, and will have to cut back.

I am the coordinator/facilitator for the Care Circle (a calling circle for singles who live alone), will be helping establish a Fibromyalgia group here in Merlin, am signed up for a three-month Master Gardener class, and, because of sending my laptop in for a new $\underline{A}$ drive, I have to completely re-type my 476-page novel. In addition to keeping up everything around here, running errands and taking care of the animals, it is time to start getting things ready for tax filing. It finally occurred to me that I am no longer Super Woman, and maybe I'd better cut back a little.

Gardening catalogs are arriving at the rate of one or two per week, and I am happily going through each one, although I really don't think I need any seeds. I have **boxes** of them, which I managed to sort into categories—herbs, vegetables, flowers, grains—and put into the computer on alphabetical charts. I hope I will be able to plant a garden this spring, but it will depend on whether we can get all of the wire, posts and miscellaneous items to enclose it. If it isn't enclosed, the deer, racoons and gophers will certainly feast on the benefits of my hard labor. Not much point in doing it just to feed the wild beasties (those other than Harry).

January 5, 2001

The installers came yesterday (Thursday) and installed our new wood stove. The owner was with them when they brought the stove in, and he commented, "Waterford is a really good stove, but an expensive one." It was a bit, but it's something we'll be living with the rest of our lives, so I'm not sorry. They finished all of the installation except the vent cap on the outside, and one of the installers said he would be back first thing this morning to do that.

When the installer arrived this morning to finish the job, he brought his son with him. "I had a birthday today, and I'm six years old," he informed me.

"Today's your birthday?" I asked.

"Last night," he confirmed. His dad said, "His birthday was yesterday, but we aren't going to celebrate it until this weekend."

The little one gave that some thought, then said, "If I have another birthday this weekend, then I'll be seven." His logic was a bit off, but his math was fine.

When they came inside the house, the installer was on his knees, partially in back of the stove, to seal the air intake pipe. His T-shirt wasn't tucked into his jeans, and there were a couple of inches of bare skin showing. Not wanting to embarrass him, I turned and walked away. His son, standing directly in back of him blurted, "Dad! You're not wearing any underwear!"

You would have been proud of me. I didn't even crack a smile. . . until they were off the property. Then, I just howled. Don't you love kids?! You never know what they are going to say. Bet his dad never takes him on another job!

We have a glider-rocker, and when Harry rocks back and forth, it squeaks. Harry said, "Schatze, quit pacing back and forth."

"You're probably driving her crazy with your squeaking."

He grinned. "Driving her crazy, or you?"

"You're working on it!"

"Good!"

"You're also working on a shorter life-span!" I warned.

Taking fair warning, he went to the garage, got some junk in a spray can (not W-D 40, but similar) and sprayed it on the movable parts. Now it creaks and groans instead of squeaking. Isn't modern technology wonderful?

I was up early this morning and privy to the opening act for today. The sky was overcast with scattered gray clouds. As the sun came up, it produced the tiniest sliver of pink against the gray clouds, then, the pink quickly increased and spread.

Gradually, it turned to peach against blue-gray clouds, and then faded to pale yellow on blue sky. God is in His Heaven! What a way to start the day.

January 11, 2001

It has taken me almost a week to get back to this letter, and probably won't get it finished until after I come home from Medford, tomorrow. I'm hoping it won't be a foggy trip.

We couldn't afford to have someone professionally prune our little orchard, so Harry got out a saw and some nippers and chopped off some branches. It still (now, more than ever), needs to be professionally pruned. It sort of looks like a Kamikaze's propeller hit some of the trees. Harry took the brush up to the meadow and stacked it in a rather high, loose, vertical pile, somewhat resembling the Leaning Tower of Pisa. It didn't look very stable. A couple of days later, I was sitting at the dining room table looking out the window when a small bird landed on top of the pile. The top half of the stack took a slow-motion, nose dive to the ground. Can you imagine that bird's surprise that he knocked over that big pile? I'll bet he thought, "Oh, boy, diet tomorrow for sure!"

Duke and Schatze were in the pasture this morning, and Duke was digging a hole. I opened the dining room window and yelled, "Duke! No!" He heard me but couldn't see me, so he kept looking around trying to locate me. When he couldn't, I guess it spooked him, and he started doing a backward retreat. He must have backed half way across that pasture, looking guilty as sin. Reminded me of a politician trying to back out of his campaign promises.

January 12, 2001

Went to Medford today to run errands and got home around 1:45 p.m. The first thing I noticed was that my "Houdini-dog" was missing. I don't know how she does it. Harry went all around the upper pasture fence with chicken wire, and she still escaped. I circled the property and checked any likely places, but couldn't find her. Later, when I was taking the stove ashes to the pasture to be dumped, I heard her whimper and discovered she was in the neighbor's back weed lot, on the north side of our property. She managed to get over there, but couldn't figure out how to get back. I don't know how long she was there, but she was glad to be rescued. My first inclination was to wring her little neck, but of course, I didn't.

Duke will be four months old tomorrow, is about half-grown and is outgrowing his puppy shyness and becoming more aggressive. He is also wreaking havoc on my potted plants. He obviously thinks they were put there for him to tip over and chew. The only option may be to hang him over the clothesline by his tail, and hang Schatze up by her ears; then, maybe I can keep the two of them out of trouble for a few minutes. Anyone want a couple of *really good* dogs? And, if you buy *that* line, I've got some *really good* swamp land in Florida I'd like to sell you.

Our new wood stove is working beautifully. I think this is the first time Harry has been warm since winter began. The stove has a cooking area on top, and yesterday, I cooked a pot of beans on it. Hope our utility bills go down a bit.

Harry is late getting home tonight, so I'm spending the quiet time writing, but I suppose I'd better put this letter to bed if I want to get it printed and mailed. God bless and keep you,

Shirlene and Harry

January 20, 2001

D ear Friends and Family,

Somebody told me that, after the holidays were over, things would slow down. They lied. The holidays went by in a pleasant whirl, but were fairly relaxing. This month has been like a carousel spinning out of control. I think I have too many irons in the fire! As usual.

The woman who wanted to organize a Fibromyalgia support group found out she was misdiagnosed and does not have FM, so I don't have to get involved in that, unless someone else requests it. (I certainly won't bring it up.)

I have now re-typed approximately 112 of the 476 pages I had to delete off my C drive when I sent my laptop in for a new A drive. Not great, but it is a start.

My Master Gardener's class started the 17th of this month, all day, every Thursday. The classroom lectures will end April 5th, but the sixty-volunteer, community hours will have to be completed sometime between April and October. They only give this class once a year, and our class is quite a large one. We have fifty-eight people, with almost as many men as women.

Our class on botany had a statement in the chapter that "roses, grapes and blackberries only live for two years." I challenge that statement. I had roses in Sacramento that had been there for 18 years, there are grape vines in Europe that have been living for centuries, and the blackberry vines on this property, I'm sure, were here before Adam and Eve. Blackberries are indestructible and eternal! I think the statement should have been that it sometimes takes two years for them to produce.

Meanwhile, back at the ranch, as they say out West. This morning, I fixed sausage, eggs, buttermilk biscuits and gravy for breakfast, cleaned up the kitchen; made applesauce, cleaned up the kitchen; baked banana nut bread, cleaned up the kitchen. I unpacked five boxes of canned goods and kitchen items, bathed the dog, did some laundry. . . and have now collapsed in my chair. Woe be unto anyone trying to pry me out of it! I'd like to think I could stay here the rest of the evening, but that would be "Alice in Wonderland." I still have to fix dinner. . . and clean up the kitchen! I didn't know how good I had it when we were remodeling, and I didn't have a kitchen to clean!

Harry has been working on the garage today and has made some noticeable differences. You can actually walk through there without a maze map. We found several things we'd been looking for, and a few things we weren't looking for. Harry is installing our old kitchen cabinets in the garage, to be used as storage and work units. The detail and amount of time he is spending on them is about comparable to the time installing our new cabinets in the kitchen. Makes me suspect he is up to something. Maybe preparing for the next time he gets into trouble and is banished to the garage?

Harry moved some insulation outside while he was cleaning inside, and Duke found it and tore it up all over the yard before he was discovered. Duke figures anything outside is fair game. When he gets into trouble and I scold him, he runs and hides in his dog house, then, he pokes his head out and peeks at me to see whether it is safe to come back out or not. He must have learned that from watching Harry.

For our anniversary, Harry got me two bouquets of flowers (made big points with that), and I got him a big box of chocolates (made BIG points with that!) which he finished off in three days. I also cooked his favorite dinner, so we both got what we liked and wanted.

When Harry comes home at night, he checks to see what I'm cooking before he decides whether he'll speak to me or not. Whoever said, "The way to a man's heart is through his stomach," certainly knew what they were talking about. Only, with Harry, it isn't a stomach, it's a bottomless pit. I don't know how anyone can eat as much as he does and still look like a refugee from a concentration camp.

After completely enclosing the upper pasture with chicken wire, Schatze-Houdini is still finding ways to escape, on a daily basis. Harry and I have both walked the pasture, but we can't find where she is getting out. The thing that worries me is that she goes up to Hugo Road (which is a fairly busy road), and people don't exactly drive slowly on it. I can't leave her in the house when I'm not here, so I've had to put her in the back orchard pen when I have to leave. Not an ideal situation, but Harry cleaned out a lot of the brush and fallen apples, so it is better than it was before.

We have been having some freezing weather at night and sometimes in the early mornings, but by early-to-mid-afternoon, the clouds or fog clears up, the sun comes out and warms everything up to forty, fifty or sixty degrees. I thought gophers went into hibernation in the winter, or maybe hitch-hiked south with the crazy geese, but no such luck. They're still here, working overtime. I was hoping this cold weather would freeze their tails off, but I think it just caused them to be more active to keep warm (and reproduce)! I read that you can get rid of them by feeding them Juicy Fruit gum, so I bought a whole carton of it. (I suspect that gardening "tip" was sponsored by Juicy Fruit.) It said Juicy Fruit was the only kind of gum that would work. Picky little devils. I suppose they are happily chewing away at this point, and they are still here.

We got our wood stove installed just before a cold spell hit, and I am happy to report it is working beautifully. As a backup, we turned our furnace down to about fifty-nine degrees, and it hasn't come on once since we have been using the wood stove. It heats the house quite well, and it has really been nice to have a cozy, warm fire. Our utility bill dropped $57.00 in the one month we've been using it.

Occasionally, when I wake up with a headache and can't sleep, I watch the sun come up over the mountains. We have a lot of high fog here, but the other morning, it was clear and cold. As the light chased the darkness away, dark, statuesque pines stood silhouetted against a backdrop of pink and purple sky. How awesome are God's wonders.

January 27, 2001

Happy Anniversary today to my kids, Kelly and Derek. Eleven years already! Happy Birthday to my Grandson, Parker, five years old today, and Happy Birthday to Harry's Mother, Elma. We're not telling her age, but probably thirty-nine—again. Way to go, Mom!

Today the clouds disappeared, the sun came out, and it got up to sixty degrees. The sun highlighted every dew-laden blade of grass before drying it off, and shot rays of light through the creek, making it sparkle like crystal as it danced, clear and cold over the rocks. A beautiful spring day in the middle of winter!

My potted tulips have poked their tips through the soil and, so far, Duke hasn't discovered them. I'm keeping my fingers crossed. Today, I caught him biting a stem off one of my roses, and I found a large stem he'd already chewed off another one. You'd think the thorns would stop him, but it doesn't seem to bother him in the slightest.

We haven't been able to find Schatze's latest escape route, so I can only let her outside when I am out watching her. Since we had such a beautiful afternoon, I took her out today for almost an hour. While she and Duke played, I walked the pasture and back yard and got my exercise.

One of the things I do while I am circling our half-acre back yard, is carry a pooper scooper shovel, and clean up some of Duke's deposits. Why is it poop from most animals—cows, horses, goats, chickens, deer, etc.—is good for fertilizer, and dog and cat poop is just something nasty to clean up? I tell you, "there *ain't* no justice!"

Duke, at four-and-one-half months and almost fifty pounds, is an automatic, high-volume, extra super-duper, pooper machine. I remember to always look down when walking in the yard. If I'm looking for piles of his calling card to clean up, I have trouble spotting them; b-u-t, just let me forget to look where I'm going, and Murphy's Law guarantees I'll step in every one of them.

I got to thinking about my job of picking up yard poop and decided I should have a title. People in charge of Corporations or companies are called CEO's (Chief Executive Officers). Garbage men are no longer garbage men, but Refuse Engineers, and janitors are now referred to as Maintenance Engineers. Using those guidelines, I believe I have come up with an appropriate title for my position. (People no longer have jobs, they have "positions.") Sooo, I have decided my title is CEO, Canine Excavation Engineer. Sounds impressive, doesn't it? You have to admit it sounds better than "person in charge of picking up the poop."

Our garage is separated from the house by a large driveway, probably fifty feet away, and I can hear Harry's stomach growling, all the way from the garage into the house. At first, I thought it was Duke growling, but no, it's Harry! Since I'm the person in charge of getting dinner and "cleaning up the kitchen," (there is probably another title in there, but I haven't had time to think about it), I'd better say goodby and fix something for Harry to eat!

Love to all,

Shirlene and Harry

February 23, 2001

Dear Friends and Family,

Spring is batting her eyelashes like a flirtatious woman, one minute weepy and wet and the next minute sunny and smiling. Foggy mornings give way to afternoons so bright the sun almost blinds. A few hours later, the skies are crying copious tears which the trees catch in their outstretched arms and slowly release on the waiting earth.

We haven't had the usual amount of rain for this area, nor snow in the surrounding mountains, so it looks like it will be a very dry, fire-prone season. I don't know how that will affect my garden, if I get to have one this year. If I do plant, I will probably have to use a lot of mulch to hold the water and keep the soil from drying out. So many things have to be done in such a short period of time, I may not get to put in a garden this year. If we can't get the fencing structure built, there's no point in planting a garden for the critters, which we seem to have in abundance.

Somewhere amid all the hullabaloo, I managed to get my pickup washed. Not that it did any good. It rained the next day. . . and the next day. . . and the next. Murphy's Law! Not enough rain to do any good, just enough to mud-splatter the pickup with road gunk. Maybe if I wash it often enough, we'll get our quota of rain for this year!

My flock of about a dozen Robins that decided to spend the winter here, patrol the front lawn like security guards, heads cocked to the side, listening for the sound of earthworms crawling through the soaked soil. (Not a true delineation, but that's what people think robins do.) A lightning strike, and Sir Robin leans back to wrest his breakfast from his personal cafeteria.

The neighbors across the creek have a flock of about twenty-five very vociferous geese that don't know they were supposed to go south for the winter, and we are directly in their daily, flight pattern. We hear them arguing back and forth as they take flight in the mornings—probably headed for the grocery store for their daily shopping—and then squabbling their way back home in the evening. *"What do you mean, I forgot the bread? You didn't put it on the list!"*

Harry's car was down for the count last week, and on Monday, I got up at 4:30 a.m. to drive him to work, (a sixty-mile round trip), which took a little over an hour. Fortunately, he arranged to ride with a co-worker until the car was fixed, so I only had to drive him ten miles to meet his ride in the morning, then pick him up at night. That's still forty miles a day for the two round trips, but better than one-hundred-twenty to make two trips a day to Central Point and back. On top of everything else I have going, it was a really *fun* way to start the day!

Harry had old "Rolls and Hardley" (*rolls* down one hill and *hardly* makes it up the next), scattered all over the garage for most of the week, but he finally got it back together and on the road again. I'm not sure the other drivers on the road appreciate that, but it was a relief for both of us! When he finished putting the car together and cleaned up the mess, he threw his oil and gasoline-soaked car rags in the trash and took them, with other items, to the burn barrel in the pasture. You guessed it! When he lit the contents and the oil rags caught, I heard a Pa-Phoom! The windows rattled, and I saw Duke slinking back to the house from the pasture. *Uh-oh! What's Harry done now?* I went to the dining room window in time to see Harry gathering up and putting out bits of burning debris scattered across the pasture. I checked to see if his insurance policies are paid up.

For those of you who were praying for me, the second mammogram showed lots of fibrous tissue and calcium deposits but no evidence of anything cancerous, and no indication of what is causing the pain. Thanks for your prayers.

Remember the old mangle ironers? You put the clothes in, smashed the lid down on top and "mangled" the wrinkles out. Well, that's what the mammogram machine reminds me of. Only I don't think it takes any wrinkles out. More likely puts a few new ones in. If you don't have a problem when you go in to get "mangled," you probably will have by the time you get out! Ouch! There is a better, gentler way, but it costs more and the insurance companies won't approve it. As usual, health care is regulated by the almighty dollar. Certainly can't have their profit margins going down!

I was supposed to schedule a treadmill test at the hospital, but I balked when I read the instructions. They informed me they would be giving me two injections of radioactive substance for the test. I said, "Oh no you won't! You're not putting that junk in my body!" so they called back yesterday and said they had scheduled the test with a cardiologist and there will be no injections. It is scheduled for March 9th. I'm sure it will be fine, but an extra prayer or two wouldn't hurt. Thanks.

March 2, 2001

The time has gone so quickly, I can't believe my Master Gardener's class is half over. The last class will be April 5th (Harry's birthday), and then all the Master Gardeners will be working furiously to get everything ready for the Spring Plant Fair and Sale, which is held every year on Mother's Day weekend—the same time that the Fairgrounds holds its Home and Garden show. The proceeds from the plant sales support the Master Gardener's program. The Fairground is within a half block of OSU's Extension office, and I am told there is transportation to shuttle people between the two events.

Each Master Gardener has a job to do at the Fair. Some sell plants, work in the kitchen, answer questions and direct people to the right areas, load plants that have been sold, or work in a booth. My job will be working the Hands On For Children booth, showing children how to plant seeds. It should be fun, and I'm looking forward to it, but I will also be glad when it is all over.

We have an assortment of teachers for our Master Gardener's classes, and most of them are very knowledgeable, present their material well, and I'm learning a lot. We have only had a couple of speakers who were as boring as watching paint dry. One man was very knowledgeable. However, he spoke fast and softly, (and carried a big stick?) ran his words together, and didn't speak into the microphone. If you were lucky, you could catch about one out of every five words he said. I thought it might be just me (dust motes in my ears?) but at the break, I heard numerous others say they couldn't understand what he was saying. Then we had the lady who not only had a boring subject, but spoke in a monotone. Wish I could have taped her. . . it was a sure-fire sleeping pill! It was amazing to look around the room and see how many people were dozing with eyes open and glazed over. OSU Extension is obviously aware of these less-than-exciting sessions, because they graciously scheduled both classes right after lunch when everyone is full, the room is warm, and the class can get a nice cat-nap until the session is over. Thoughtful of them! That way, after our break, we were all refreshed and ready for the last speaker of the day.

I work in the greenhouse at the Extension Office every Tuesday afternoon, and I am in class all day Thursday. On Monday I run errands, and our Bible study is on Wednesday. That only leaves Friday and Saturday to clean house, pay bills or do computer work, do laundry, clean up the property, or anything else that needs to be done. Not enough hours in the day, or days in the week, but I suppose if there were more, I'd find some way of over-filling those days also.

I came home Tuesday to find Schatze gone from her pen—again. I heard yip, yip and noticed that Duke was in our pasture, at the fence, nose to nose with Romeo, my neighbor's horse. Duke does not go "yip, yip," so I figured Schatze must be up there someplace. Right! She was in the neighbor's pasture with Romeo and couldn't figure out how to get back home, and Romeo was leaning down to sympathize while Duke supervised. I blocked the hole where she got out, but she found another way out the next day and was in the pasture, again, with Romeo. Same song, second verse!! Harry nailed up more boards along the fence line, but I wouldn't place any bets on her not finding another way out.

As for Duke, he has gotten big enough that the three-foot drop off into the creek presents no problem at all for him. When I don't see him anywhere on the property, I can usually figure he is wading in the creek. He considers it his own private kiddie wading pool, and the cold water doesn't bother him one bit. He also considers my rose bushes and other plants his gourmet appetizers. One of the women in my Bible study class innocently suggested I get him some chew toys. HA! She came home with me after Bible study and saw the front yard strewn with miscellaneous toys and big dog bones. In Duke's eyes, that has nothing whatsoever to do with my plants. And he loves the little aluminum labels I put on everything. I think he samples the labels so he will know which plant to eat next. All of my labels have been removed, chewed into mangled balls, and the little blobs of aluminum placed discreetly around the yard. I haven't a clue as to what I have planted. Oh, yes, I can identify blueberries, but which variety? Destructive and expensive! I'm trying to be patient, but if he doesn't outgrow this, I'm going to pack his bags and send him down the road! On days when I find my planters tipped over and prized plants scattered about the yard, I'd gladly give him to the first vagrant passing by. When he has an occasional good day, and he comes bounding up to me with his big puppy smile and soft brown eyes, I wouldn't sell him for $500.00. (However, don't tempt me with an offer!)

Duke will be six-months old the 13th of this month, and he is getting really big. I think the man who gave him to me lied about his breed. I have recently decided he is 50% charging rhino, 25% kangaroo, 25% Percheron, 10% Einstein, and 5% Mongolian idiot! Yes, I know that totals more than 100%, but with Duke, that's appropriate.

I had hoped he would be a good watch dog, but I think his priorities are a little confused. My *neighbor,* Jo, came over the other evening to return a couple of my dishes, and Duke barked and growled at her. (However, he did it from the security of *inside* his dog house.) She came to the door, petted him and talked to him. The next day when the UPS man—a *complete stranger*—came to the door with a package, Duke greeted him with wagging tail and bounding joy, and not a "Wuff" in sight! Some watch dog!

The birds returned yesterday, right on cue, as if they knew the first of March is supposed to be spring. They have been acting twitter-pated and checking out the bird houses, which have not as yet been cleaned out and replaced. Last year's old nests are still in them! Where did the time go?

Last night, Harry told me he had completed the protection box for my Mason Bees. . . and today I found that they have already started hatching out! Too early, too early! Go back in the nest! There's not a thing blooming for them to survive on. I guess you could say that this weekend, Harry and I will be busy with the birds and the bees! I figure it's time Harry learns about these things.

God bless and keep you. Sending our love, until next time,

Shirlene & Harry

March 20, 2001

Dear Friends & Family,

This year is flying by with the speed of a rocket shot into space. Spring is almost here and I don't know where the time has gone. Even though it is my favorite time of year, I can't say I'm ready for it. I had hoped to have my garden area built, fenced and ready for planting, but no such luck. I have plants sprouted in the living room, transplants in the den, and am running out of room. If I don't get some kind of miracle, I won't have any place to plant them. Maybe in Harry's bathroom?

All of our cat, dog and bird food is stored in large, forty-gallon trash barrels with lock-on lids, under the RV carport in back of the garage. Because the area is sand and small gravel, it is Schatze's (and the cat's) favorite "potty" area. A few nights ago when I filled the cat's two-gallon feeder, I forgot to put the lid back on the cat food. Next evening when I took Schatze for her last walk before bedtime, I noticed that the lid was off the barrel. I shined the light *at* the barrel, so I could see to put the lid on, and something moved inside it. *Uh-oh, there's a cat in there, helping himself.* I poked at the barrel with the rake handle, thinking the cat would jump out, but it didn't. I shined the light inside the barrel and realized it wasn't a cat. It was a possum, and it wasn't about to jump out of that barrel with me standing there and a crazy little terrier ready to attack. I knew Schatze would attack if it jumped out, and she certainly wouldn't be a match for a possum, so I put the lid on the barrel, picked up Schatze and locked her in the house. I went back, took the lid off and shook the barrel a couple of times, but other than hissing at me, the possum didn't move. I guess I interrupted his dinner and he wasn't about to leave until he had dessert. I decided discretion was the better part of valor, wished the possum Bon Appetite´ and came back in the house. Next morning the possum was gone, having dined lavishly on my cat food. He didn't even leave a tip! I put the lid on securely and locked it in place!

The birds are back, completely twitter-pated and doing their aerial mating dance. I love to watch the tiny Swallows dive and turn. They are so fast! I'm hoping we can attract enough Swallows to eat at least part of the beetle population that has hatched out.

Some of the bird houses are cleaned and back up, mounted on metal poles. It may not completely deter the cats but at least the poor little birds have a sporting chance. The Swallows and Sparrows are fighting over the few birdhouses we have ready and apparently the Sparrows are winning. I saw a Sparrow carrying bits of straw and grass into the house she has claimed, and she hasn't even paid her deposit or first and last month's rent! Nervy little tweeter!

Mischief is really ticked off at me. She caught a Robin and I heard it screaming, so I dashed outside, grabbed her and made her turn it loose. She hadn't yet had a chance to cripple it, and it flew away. Boy, was she mad. She glared at me. *I caught that bird fair and square. Butt out!* Harry had also rescued one of her catches a couple of weeks before, so now she's getting sneaky. Yesterday when I went into the garage to get some paper towels, there were bird feathers inside the old cabinets Harry installed in the garage. They are open on the end and the cats can get in there, so Mischief took her catch and hid while she ate it. Just left the messy evidence.

I took Duke to the Vet last week and had his voice raised an octave. Now he won't be able to produce any puppies and that's a big relief. With *my* luck, whoever had the female would dump the whole litter on me. Can't you just see me with six or eight "Dukes?" Aaaauuuuugh! The scream would be heard from here to California! At six months old, Duke weighs sixty-five pounds, and still growing. Must be all my plants he's been eating. He's obviously a gourmet who figures he needs some 'salad' to go with his dinner.

All thirteen of our little dwarf and semi-dwarf fruit trees are now planted and ready to bud. In fact, the Nectarine is already blooming and the blossoms smell sweet enough to eat.

We probably won't get any fruit for a couple of years, but at least, the trees are finally out of those large planters and into their permanent home!

Meanwhile, back at the Funny Farm. . . I had a pleasant and quiet birthday last Sunday (18th) and when I figured up how old I was, (I can never remember. Thirty-nine?) I was delighted to discover I was a year younger than I thought. How about that? I got to *legally* deduct a year. I've been deducting for years, but this one was legitimate! Unfortunately, that good news was followed up this morning by some I'd rather not have heard.

The doctor's office called and told me the stress test came back, shows some abnormalities, possibly blocked arteries but they are not sure to what extent, and they are scheduling an appointment with a Cardiologist for some further tests. The EKG indicated damage to the heart muscle. Not exactly the best "Happy Birthday" message I received. I've suspected for some time that there was a problem, but having it confirmed didn't exactly make my day. I'm not worried or panicky for it is in God's hands, but if you have a church prayer chain, I would appreciate being on it for a while.

I had to drop my Tuesday afternoon work at the OSU Extension Greenhouse, and they were really nice about it. I will probably not try to put in extra hours until this summer, after the classes are over. Only three more Thursday classes and we are through. Unless something comes up, I still plan on working at the Spring Plant Sale on Mother's Day weekend. I can do that one sitting at a table, so that should work out all right. Then maybe I can work a few hours in the office at the Plant Clinic later this summer, after all the other hubbub is over.

March 21, 2001

I think we skipped spring and went right into summer. It was eighty degrees here today. I hope that is not an omen of what is yet to come. I moved up here to get away from the heat. Actually, it is only about ten degrees cooler here than Sacramento, so it was probably around ninety degrees there today.

I planted lots of daffodils last fall and a few are blooming, but I had a lovely surprise. Someone who lived here before also planted daffodils, and they bloomed before the ones I planted, so I've had fresh flowers in the house. Lovely.

Best sign off and get this ready to mail. Thanks for your prayers,

Shirlene and Harry

April 25, 2001

Dear Friends & Family,

Spring! My favorite time of year. Like the proverbial mermaid that darted in and out of the waves, luring sailors to their destruction, Spring has darted in and out of our area, luring unwary gardeners to put seeds in the soil so She can dump six inches of snow on top of everything the day the new shoots appear above ground. Actually, I don't think they've had six inches of snow in this area in *many* years, but I know if I planted my garden ahead of schedule, it would happen, so I'll wait (impatiently) for May 15 before I plant. I wouldn't want to be the cause of a blizzard!

We are having a typical April. Rain one day and sun the next, or bits of each in the same day. Temperatures in the eighties and nineties for a couple of days and then back down to freezing and fog. In spite of the goofy weather, the mountains are marching into spring dressed in rain-washed blues and greens and carrying bouquets of forsythia and wildflowers. The lawn is polka-dotted with dandelions and accented with a rainbow of daffodils and tulips. What a vibrant splash of colors! When the tulips were closed, they looked like colorful Easter eggs on long sticks.

The trees dressed in their Easter finery of pink and white blossoms, and the daffodils and tulips shouted joyous exclamations! The house has been full of tulip and daffodil arrangements, perfumed with hyacinths. Their color and fragrance really lifted my soul. Unfortunately, they've passed their blooming stage now, and I'm without fresh flowers. That's like an addict being without a fix!

Harry dug holes that were strangely reminiscent of large gophers, and we planted rosebushes and peonies along the driveway. I asked Harry to be careful not to disturb the dirt ball around the largest peony we transplanted from the back, and by the time it was in the ground, he had managed to completely lose all the soil around the roots. The poor thing still hasn't recovered, and it's been almost two weeks. It *was* a beautiful bush, but now, it is lying on the ground looking anemic, like it needs a shot of elixir.

I bought two *Pieris Japonica* (Mountain Fire) bushes, and we planted them next to the Mason Bee house so they would have a constant supply of food. The bees started hatching out before anything was in bloom, and some of them died. Not all hatched, so maybe the ones that are now hatching will be able to propagate the colony. I hope so. They are great little pollenizers. Much better than honey bees, and they don't sting. Of course, they also don't make honey. Oh, well.

121

Harry cleared the blackberry bushes from the back of the property, a monumental job, and now we can not only see the creek, we can walk down to it. The creek is so pretty, and it is so nice to have that area open; however, it will be a continual fight to keep the blackberries from filling in again. I think blackberries were probably part of man's punishment for the Garden of Eden mess up. Eventually, I want to landscape that area with Dogwood trees, forsythia, ferns, hostas, coleus, bleeding hearts, cyclamen and other shade-loving plants. It will probably take three or four years, but someday that could be a really beautiful area.

When we looked at the property last summer, the black-berries were full and thick. This winter when they started dying out, we discovered that someone had thrown a couple of old tires under those brambles. As the canes and leaves died back, I counted seven or eight tires; then thirteen. When Harry cut back all the canes, we had a grand total of *twenty-seven* old tires, some miscellaneous junk and an old Christmas tree. Evidently, the previous owners or the renters used that area as their own private dump site and just let the blackberries cover it. It will cost us $69.00 to get rid of all the old tires!

Harry started working the night shift March 26th and will probably continue through the summer. He leaves here around 2:15 p.m., goes to work at 3:00 p.m., and gets off at 1:00 a.m. He took a week of vacation last week and got the electrical installed for the driveway gate, and installed a garage door opener on one of our garage doors. We bought two garage door openers, but installed one of them on the gate. Much cheaper than the regular gate openers, and works just as well.

The doctor's office finally called to tell me my Cardi-ologist appointment is May 1st. I originally went to the doctor about the chest pains, lack of breath, etc., January 17th and they can't get me in to *talk* to a Cardiologist until *May 1?!* I told the receptionist, "Well, I'll either be healed or dead by then." She just laughed. If I were a man, I'd have been ushered in post-haste. My uncle went in with the same symptoms a couple of years ago, and they jumped on it instantly. Another uncle went in a couple of weeks ago with the same symptoms, and they rushed him through immediately. Being a woman, it isn't taken very seriously. It can wait three or four months.

I won't know the complete story until the May 1st appointment, but my GP doctor said from the test he now has, I've had a heart attack. I was relatively sure that had happened, and I can even tell him the *date* it happened—the night after I had spent thirteen straight hours unloading the two trucks, when we moved up here.

You can't see the bend in the creek from our bank, so I put on my rubber boots and waded up the creek. The rocks were slippery, so I had to take my time and step carefully, but Duke and I made it almost to the bend. I stopped a little short of the bend because it looked like the water was deep enough to go over the top of my boots. We have such a nice creek, and it flows all year long. Of course, it also brings in the critters—racoons, possums and deer. Duke thinks it's his private wading and drinking pool, and now that the blackberry vines are cleared, Schatze and the cats go down to the water to drink. I just go down to look and listen.

Although everyone enjoyed the Master Gardener class and we learned a lot, when it ended on April 12th, we were all ready for it to be over. Now, we will have our plant sale Mother's Day weekend, and then I will be working in the MG clinic answering phones, on and off during the summer until I get my sixty hours of volunteer time put in.

Jo Durham and I found a new discount grocery store in Medford. We just went in to "look around." When we got back out I said, "Are you a bad influence on me, or am I a bad influence on you?"

Jo said, "How much did you spend?"

"Fifty-nine dollars. How about you?"

She laughed. "Fifty-nine dollars."

Obviously, we're a bad influence on each other. I love it!

I'd better close and get this printed if I'm going to get it in the mail tomorrow. Sending best wishes your way, as ever,

Shirlene and Harry

May 5, 2001

Dear Friends & Family,

Thank You, Thank You, *Thank You,* **Thank You!!** In all the ways that it is possible to say it, ***Thank you*** for your prayers. There is no force on earth as powerful as the power of prayer, and when prayer warriors storm the gates of heaven, miracles still happen.

When I first went to the doctor because I was having some problems, my blood pressure was 175/96, which the nurse said was getting a bit too high. My first EKG showed that there had probably been a heart attack, and my treadmill test indicated the possibility of some blocked arteries. I was also having erratic heart beats.

In between the first group of tests and the last ones, I requested prayer, and I know some of you not only prayed for me, but put me on your prayer chain at church. When I went for this last group of tests, there was no indication of a heart attack (but some damage to the heart muscle?), and there were no blocked arteries. Prayer works.

The doctor said there was some damage to the front of the heart muscle, and damaged or torn muscles in the chest surrounding the heart. That happened when we moved up here, and I did thirteen hours of heavy lifting, unloading the two trucks. Those muscles haven't healed because of the Fibromyalgia, and I'm also still having irregular heart beats. But, Praise God, those are things I can work with. Not nearly as serious as the first tests indicated.

I've been closely watching what I eat and have been using some pickled garlic, herbs and supplements to control my blood pressure, which is now down around 133/74, 147/83, 130/70, etc. Most of the time under 140/80, so it has been very good. The doctor was amazed that I did it without medication. (Best of all, no side affects!) I just started pulling my reference books off the shelf and researching everything I could find on heart and blood pressure. I'm taking Hawthorn (heals the heart muscle,) garlic (thins the blood,) Salmon oil (Omega 3 fatty acids,) E (healing,) Ginkgo (improves blood flow, irregular heartbeats,) and Coenzyme Q10 (helps mitochondria of the cell work more efficiently, especially in the heart).

I could still use prayer for the irregular heartbeats be-cause I get tired and out of breath very easily, and of course, for the Fibromyalgia, which is a real pain-in-the . . . muscles! Ha, thought I was going to say something else, didn't you? But, along with the prayer request, lots of praising God and thankfulness. God is good!

The Bible says that David danced with joy before the Lord, and I know exactly how he felt! When I came out of the doctor's office, I was doing a little "Snoopy dance" all the way home. Again, thanks for your prayers.

May 17, 2001

As you can see, I actually started this letter just after my Cardiologist appointment, but things got rather hectic here, and I didn't get it finished and in the mail. I got involved in getting ready for the Master Gardener's Spring Plant Fair which took place last weekend. And this week, I have been trying to catch up on things around here (a never-ending task,) getting ready for my kids who will be visiting this weekend. *Hectic* would pretty well describe my life. I guess that's better than boring.

Although the Spring Plant Fair was somewhat chaotic, I really enjoyed it. My contribution was working at the Hands On For Kids table, showing children how to plant a seed. Chet's, one of Grants Pass' local nurseries, donated some seed, peat pots and planting mix. I had nasturtium, sunflower, pumpkin and popcorn seeds for the kids to plant, and they could choose which one they wanted to plant, then take it home. Upon explaining the choice to one eight-year-old boy, his eyes got wide with disbelief. "I didn't know you could *grow* popcorn!" Evidently, he thought you only got it at grocery stores and movie theaters. Aren't kids great?

I had all ages during the two days we ran the plant fair, and most were really delightful. I had one set of three-year-old twins whose eyes lit up like sparklers when they pushed their seed into the planting mix and then got to take it home. But, the one that touched my heart the most was a seventeen-year-old, mentally retarded boy who passed the table several times, watching what was going on. Finally, I called out to him, "Would you like to come and plant a seed?" His grin was as big

Today, I was vacuuming and moved the living room chair away from the window. Schatze was in the dining room chair, and when the birds flew toward the front of the house, she raced to the living room and jumped for the chair—which wasn't there. S-p-l-a-t! Right against the wall. Didn't even slow her down.

Schatze has a ball a little bit larger than a man's fist, that has indentations in it so she can carry it around. The other day she was across the room from the ball, stalking it as intently as if it were a game bird. She reared back on her haunches, then sprang like a baby fawn, *boing, boing, boing, pounce,* on top of the ball. When her front feet hit the ball, it rolled to the side and sent her sprawling. She jumped to her feet and whirled around in a circle, looking for the attacker. Her expression said, *"Who did that to me?"* Since I was across the room cracking up, she thought I must be guilty, and she gave me a dirty look. One thing about having animals, you never lack for entertainment.

Again, thank you for your prayers. Don't quit. With prayer, it is possible to be healed of the erratic heartbeats and whatever else is there. What a mighty God we serve! And know that I am continually praying for you. My prayer list has approximately sixty-five people on it—all of my friends and family—and I try to pray for each person on a regular, weekly basis. I may not know your exact needs, but God does—and you are truly, always in my prayers.

I suppose if I'm going to get this in the mail tomorrow, I'd better quit writing and get busy printing and mailing. My love, as always,

Shirlene and Harry

May 28, 2001

D ear Friends and Family,

A year ago this weekend, we were on the road, moving to Oregon. I usually try to stay off the road on any major holiday weekend, and moving is definitely *not* something I would recommend. However, somehow, we survived it and have been here a year that has zipped by like greased lightning.

Harry is working hard, trying to get the garden enclosure finished, I suspect as much for his sake as mine. I know he will be thrilled to be finished with it! (Let's not tell him I have ten other projects lined up when he is finished with this one!) I have half-grown seedlings that have been transplanted a couple of times, on tables in the den, and some moved out to the back deck, all waiting for the garden area to be completed. I'm not complaining though, because the garden enclosure is a BIG project, and Harry has done everything in his power to get it completed. It will get done when it gets done, and the plants will get planted, whenever. If I don't have time for a full garden this year, there's always next year.

I managed to plant a small 7' x 12' back-yard plot. Since space was limited, I crammed as much as possible into that small area. Talk about intensive gardening! I divided it into two-foot plots and planted beets, parsley, onions, chives, three kinds of lettuce, spinach, endive, kale, French Tarragon, Rosemary, one Peaches and Cream hollyhock, one shoo-fly plant, and one bean that I am growing for seed.

This past week, I made three hanging baskets, filled them with Nasturtiums and hung them from the front porch rafters. I also potted three bright-colored geraniums in white pots and put them on the porch rail. They probably won't bloom for three or four more weeks, but when they do, they should be really colorful.

I had some beautiful iris blooms, in spite of the ones Duke ate. I couldn't tell you the names of the ones that bloomed because Duke also chewed up all the tags. My roses are just now starting to bloom, but if the heat keeps up, they will quit. It will probably take me a couple of years to get things planted so that I have continuous flowers from February-March through November-December, but that is my eventual goal.

I'm also keeping busy with cooking, cleaning, inside and outside maintenance, watering and weeding, and taking care of the animals which now includes our goat, Clementine. There's never a moment when there is nothing to do. Each time I look out the window, I wonder, *why do weeds grow at three times the rate of vegetables, flowers and useful plants?* What this place needs is a couple of twenty-thirty-some-things, full-time work horses. What is *has* is a couple of pooped-out old seniors, working whenever the Spirit calls and the worn-out body is able to answer. About the equivalent of having an eight-cylinder car, hitting on four cylinders. Part of the problem is, the iron in our blood has turned to lead in our butts.

Weather-wise, this has been a perfect weekend. Partially cloudy with a light breeze, keeping the temperature around seventy-two degrees. My kind of weather. Since Harry has been working outside cementing posts for the garden enclosure, he would probably agree that it is his kind of weather, too.

We've had several days in May that were over one-hundred degrees. I'm afraid we're in for a long, hot summer and probably a lot of fires. They've already stopped all outside burning, and burning in covered barrels requires a permit, and is restricted to the end of June. Hope we don't run out of water before the end of the summer. I don't know how far down the water table is, or how deep our well is, but we really have to be careful not to water too long, or we run out of water.

When I brought Clementine home, Harry put a three-foot fence across the end of the orchard area where the shed is located, to keep Clementine away from the fruit trees, most of which would be toxic for her. Clementine is a little Nigerian Dwarf, only about 15" high. However, keep in mind that Clementine is a **g-o-a-t!** Goats climb. Goats jump! And goats escape. Does that tell you that a three foot fence doesn't hold her?

After Clementine had been here about a week, Harry knocked on the door and I went to see what he wanted. He said, "Would you like to come out and catch your goat?" He had tried to coax and call her, but she wouldn't get near enough for him to catch her. I went outside and called her, she came right to me, and I led her back to the pen. She had pushed her way under the bottom of the fence. Harry re-enforced the bottom with boards and nailed the fence to it. Next escape, she was at the front door, ba-aah-ing for me to come out and pet her. (Goats are very social.) This time, she had jumped the fence. Harry extended the fence to five feet.

Harry just came to the door, laughing. "Clementine just found a new way to escape." Her food is stored in a plastic trash can with a lock-down lid, sitting next to the gate. The trash can is about three feet high—a nice jump for a little goat. Clementine hopped up on top of the trash can, and the remaining two-foot leap over the top of the fence was noooo prob-lem. Piece of cake! We moved the food can away from the fence, and Clementine baa-ahed her disapproval. The trash can lid *was* rounded on top, but Clementine has re-designed it to concave!

I am taking care of a friend's dog while she is in Southern California for a week. I told Harry, "I have two Dingy

Dogs, two Crazy Cats, and one Goofy Goat." He looked at me with the expectancy of one who is waiting for the other shoe to drop. "At least that list didn't include me this time."

"Don't push your luck! I'm not through yet!"

Derek, Kelly and my grandkids, Brantley and Parker, came to visit last weekend. After being confined to a city apartment most of the time, this huge back yard got a thorough breaking-in by two running, chasing, exuberant kids. They played tag, ran in circles, chased the dog, were chased *by* the dog, visited the goat, walked down to the stream, and swung on the swing that hangs from the big oak. And that was just the first hour they were here!

On Sunday we went to church. Then, Sunday afternoon, Kelly, the kids and I spent about half the afternoon wading in the creek, skipping stones, dodging crawdads, and building dams that didn't do one thing to impede the flow of water, but probably built a memory that will last a lifetime. On Monday morning, before they loaded up the van to go home, we hooked up the wagon behind the yard tractor, filled the bottom with straw, covered it with an old sheet, and took them on a "hay" ride all around the property. This is a great place for kids.

We have a couple of small-town newspapers, and I love reading the ads. One section advertises free animals. A couple of weeks ago there was an ad that read, "One-year-old, male, neutered, partially house-broken **Datsun.**" Hmmm, a partially-house broken car! And neutered, yet. Such a deal.

Another ad read, "Bearly used beds..." As in Goldilocks and the Three Bears??

Did you know that the Bible has the first recorded in-stance of salt-pork? In Matthew 8:32, when the swine ran into the sea. Okay, so it's corny. I didn't make it up, I read it someplace. *You* come up with something!

I read some cute jokes I'd like to pass on. A Sunday school teacher was discussing the Ten Commandments with her five and six-year-olds. After explaining the commandment to "honor thy father and thy mother," she asked, "Is there a commandment that teaches us how to treat our brothers and sisters?" Without missing a beat, one little boy, the oldest in the family, answered, "Thou shalt not kill."

One more and I'll quit. A six-year-old girl was sitting in church with her four-year-old brother, who talked out loud, sang, and giggled. Finally, she told him to be quiet. "Why? Who's going to stop me?" She pointed to the back of the church. "See those two men standing back there? They're hushers."

'Nuff, already! Love, prayers and all that good stuff, 'till next time.

Shirlene and Harry

Wednesday, July 4, 2001

Dear Friends and Family,

I don't know what happened to the month of June, but I lost it somewhere. I probably put it down someplace and couldn't remember where I left it. Ah, yes, another "Senior Moment!" Now if I can just figure out what to do with July, and get it done before I misplace this month.

As of the 24th of this month, I will start working at the University of Oregon Extension Office, six hours, one day a week, to complete my Master gardeners pay-back hours. We donate sixty hours of community service, and I only have thirty-one at this point, so the clinic will be a good way to complete my hours. I wonder if they know that they're taking an awful chance? After I work there, the clinic may never be the same again!

Last week we had a lovely rain, and God gave everything a good soaking, but by this week, you'd never know it happened. However, everything is blooming in its season. We now have bright, orange Day Lilies at the ends of the Iris bed, and a six-foot tall mullein plant in the same bed. I know mullein is considered a weed, but it is also an herb, so I left it growing in the flower bed. I rather like the plant, and the hummingbirds love the yellow flowers that surround the top of the stalk.

The tall *stems* of mullein were once burned as tapers in funeral processions. (Isn't that just what you always wanted to know?) The *flowers* can be made into tinctures, salves, infusions (tea), syrup and oils, and have been used for chronic, dry coughs, throat inflammations, wounds, hemorrhoids and eczema. The *leaves*, made into an infusion, can be used for chronic coughs and throat inflammations, and to promote sweating, or made into a tincture and combined with other herbs for respiratory disorders. The leaves were also made into tobacco and smoked for asthma and tuberculosis. There you go! With that helpful hint, you can cut your tobacco costs!

We have one, possibly two hummingbird families that fight over our three feeders. There is plenty of food for all, but they are territorial little dickenses, so they zoom and fight. Our Swallows are still zooming and diving and driving Schatze crazy, and the Sparrows are mating for their third set of babies this summer. Horny little devils! I would tell you this place is for the birds, but we have critters as well, so I guess it's more like a three-ring-circus. Or, if you include the human inhabitants, it could be classified as a looney-bin or funny-farm.

Tuesday, July 17, 2001

Obviously, I didn't get this finished and in the mail, so I'll try again. We've had some really goofy weather here, but I guess no more than the rest of the country. We had a number of thunder and lightning storms, which terrified Schatze and kept her so close to me I thought she was attached with Velcro, but no more rain, except for enough sprinkles to make things very humid. If I didn't know better, I'd have thought I was living in the South, or maybe Texas or the East Coast. Humid, you can have!

I've decided I hate making business phone calls. You never reach a person, just a recorded "menu." I resent the word "menu" used with telephone selection. If we're going to talk menus, then I want someone to take my order, and I expect to be served something to eat (a vegi-burger with potato salad, please.) And the *voice!!* Hold your nose and talk, and you've got the sound! Where do they find these bimbos? I think it must be the same person, doing all the recording, nationwide.

Remember talent contests? Well, the choice of the person doing the recordings was decided by a talent-less contest, and the rules were as follows:

1) You must be able to talk in a monotone with absolutely no voice inflection.

2) You must be **ten** of the world's most boring people, rolled into one package.

3) You must have the world's worst sinus problems and must talk through your nose.

I'm sure there are more talent-less rules than those I mentioned, but you get the idea.

A well-known, financial brokerage firm, (unfortunately, I don't know which one—I heard this second-hand) has a recording with a number of selections. If you do not choose one by the time they reach the end of their selections, they say, "If you want to hear a duck quack, press 7." The caller presses 7, and sure enough, there is a duck quacking. Then the phone disconnects. Ah, finally, someone with a little class! I wish I knew which firm, because I would call it just to hear something other than the standard monotone garbage.

Other things that bug me are all the nagging things our technology has invented. Back in 1983, my (then) husband bought a car that talked to you. (Recording done by the same monotone ding-bat!) If you had the door open when the key was in the ignition, Miss Monotone would say, "The-door-is-open! The-door-is-open! The-door-is-open!" repeatedly, until you closed the lousy door. Driving down the freeway at 65 MPH, listening to the radio, suddenly the radio kicks off and Miss Monotone's voice fills the car. "Your-windshield-washer-fluid-is-low." This was repeated at least three times before the radio came back on. You found yourself yelling back at her, "Who the heck cares?" I don't think that talking car phase lasted very long, and I can understand why. Who wants a nagging car?

An-n-d, how about nagging appliances. The clock radio nags you to get up in the morning. Even if it is a nice program, it's still nagging. *Go away, leave me alone. I don't want to get up!* Then there's the microwave dinging, telling me my tea water is ready, the kitchen timer buzzer, telling me I'm supposed to be taking care of *something* if I could only remember what it was. The dryer nags me to take the clothes out and fold them, my car buzzes if I leave the keys in the ignition or the lights on (I'm okay with that last one,) and fire alarms go off when I'm cooking. We live in a nagging world!

The corny joke section of this letter: Why did the frog say "meow"? He was learning a foreign language.

I read a statistic that said, "If you retired today, you could live quite comfortably until about 3:00 p.m. tomorrow." By Jove, I think they finally got something right!

Don't worry about me *suffering* from senility. I'm enjoying every minute of it!

I know you were expecting me to report on some thrilling adventure, but there isn't much going on around here, just the usual exciting things like watching the grass grow, so I'll leave you with the "cliff-hanger" of wondering what the next letter will bring.

My love and prayers,

Shirlene and Harry

P.S. My granddaughter had a birthday on the 12th of this month.

Happy ninth birthday, Brantley!

Saturday, July 28, 2001

Dear Friends & Family,

Half way through the summer and no relief in sight. The drought continues. The rock bed of our beautiful little creek is as dry as bones in the desert, with only one or two little puddles where the deeper pools had been. It takes almost constant watering to keep alive the yard and flowers and the few vegetables I planted in two small beds. I wonder if our well will hold out? If that goes dry, we're in big trouble. I never thought I'd see the day when I'd look forward to winter, but if it brings the rains, I'm ready. Unfortunately, the national weather service thinks we will have yet another dry year, but they only report the weather. The Weather Maker, the Producer of this show, is a personal Friend of mine, and we're on very good speaking terms. What we really need is some good, prayer warriors, praying for rain and a good snow pack this winter, so we'll have spring and summer run-off. We so often "miss the boat" because we fail to take it to Him in prayer. We have not, because we ask not.

I was watering the little fruit trees we planted in the pasture area a couple of nights ago, and I glanced over the fence at the vacant lot north of us. A doe was placidly grazing among the dry weeds. She stopped and looked at me and, deciding I was not a threat, went on with her grazing. We watched one another for ten or fifteen minutes before she finally disappeared through the blackberry brambles, into the creek.

A couple of days prior, Schatze went into a frenzy at the living room window. I glanced outside to see what had her blood pressure up, and spotted a quail family, two adults and seven or eight small quails, zig-zagging across our front lawn and driveway. I rushed to the door and got Harry's attention. Although he was working at the west end of the drive, he would have never glanced up and seen them. They crouched low, scurried across the lawn and drive, and the babies hid in the grass by the fence while the adults perched on top of the fence, checking for danger on the other side.

Yesterday, on the way to Medford to shop, I spotted a family of wild turkeys along side of I-5. I've heard wild turkeys in the woods but have never seen them before, so that was a real thrill. I guess the drought is driving a lot of animals out of hiding, searching for food and water.

Every evening, from about 7:00 p.m. to 9:30 or 10:00 p.m., I am outside watering. The ground that was watered and looked so wet the night before is dry and cracked, dried out by the wind and baked hard by the hot sun. Keeping the grass green is a losing battle. There are patches of green struggling to survive, with brittle brown patches encroaching like an oil spill on the ocean. The only thing that isn't bothered by the drought is the weeds. They flourish anytime.

I was checking out of Wal-Mart earlier today, and I happened to be at the counter where the cigarettes were sold. When I saw the prices, I almost fainted! Some cartons were thirty-plus dollars, and the on-sale cartons were $26.99! Two smokers in a household could soon burn up enough money to buy a new home, a new car, a trip to Hawaii—whatever! I quit smoking thirty-eight years ago when they went up to a quarter a pack. Not going to pay *that* kind of price! I figured I was burning good money, and that was outrageous!

I stood beside an elderly woman yesterday at Costco, while she complained to the pharmacist about the cost of her medicine, which was $43.00 for a month's supply. She said, "I can't afford that!" Later, as I was leaving, she was getting into her car, parked next to my pickup. I was feeling sorry for her, not being able to afford her medicine, until I saw her bumper sticker. It said, "I smoke and I vote." There's a message in there. Think about it.

Harry and I went to Crater Lake last Sunday. Harry had never been there, but I was there twenty-five years ago. I had forgotten how steep the walls of that crater are. It's a loong way down! There is only one place to get down to the lake, and that is a steep, one mile hike, one way. Crater Lake is the deepest lake in the United States, and I think the third deepest in the world. Beautiful lake. There is a thirty-three mile drive you can take around the rim of the lake, but we didn't have time for it this trip. Maybe next time.

Sunday, July 29, 2001

This morning when I took Schatze out for her morning 'constitutional,' a two-prong buck was grazing in the back yard, out by the creek. He looked at me as though I was intruding in his territory, but as long as I stood still, he continued to browse. The deer are coming to the low areas in search of water, and we have little to offer.

I've been praying for rain, and right now it is sprinkling, even though the weather forecasters said there would be <u>no chance</u> of rain. I'm going to keep praying because what we need is a good, old-fashioned gully-washer! The Bible says, "*And all things, whatsoever ye shall ask in prayer,* believing, *ye shall receive.*" (Matt: 21:22) We need to ask in faith.

Today, after church, we went to Galice, which is about 11 miles from us, up Merlin-Galice road. We drove "through" it once before, which is quite easy to do. You arrive at, literally, a wide spot with a lodge on the east side of the road. There is a sign on the lodge that says. ***This Is Galice.*** That's all there is. There ain't no mo'! One building constitutes the entire "town" of Galice! Now, don't tell me *we* don't have exciting things to do and places to see!

At the back of the lodge, overlooking the Rogue River, is a huge deck with about thirty picnic tables where you can watch the sunburned, river rafters while you share your lunch with the yellow jackets. The food was good, but I could have done without the yellow jackets! They weren't trying to sting us, just get into our food, which made it a little difficult to eat. Yellow jacket hors d'oeuvre, anyone?

Each evening, just as the last remnant of dusk fades into night, I get into the spa (on the back deck) and watch the stars come out of hiding while the crickets serenade me. After a half hour of soothing water massage, I come back in for Bible study before going to bed. What a way to end the day!

I found something you might enjoy, so I"m sending you this list of Top Ten Old Folks Party Games, in case you might be doing any entertaining.

1. Sag, You're it!

2. Pin the Toupee on the Bald Guy.

3. Kick the Bucket

4. Twenty Questions Shouted into Your Good Ear

5. Doc, Doc, Goose

6. Red Rover, Red Rover, The Nurse Says Bend Over

7. Hide and Go Pee

8. Simon Says Something Incoherent

9. Spin the Bottle of Mylanta

10. Musical Recliners

Some of us can relate! Until next time, my love and prayers,

Shirlene and Harry

Monday, August 13, 2001

Dear Friends and Family,

Our weather here has been like a lot of other places across the nation—unreasonably hot! I think we've probably set some records. Last week we had 106, 108, and 110 degree temperatures. I usually go out and work in the yard and do my watering in the late evening from 7:00 - 9:30 p.m., but it was so hot, even after the sun went down, that I couldn't stay out very long. The heat makes me sick, so I'll be glad to see cooler weather and, hopefully, some rain. We've had a couple of sprinkles during the summer, but not enough to get the ground wet. We only had one good rain, and that was in June. Nothing since. With no snow pack in the mountains, our creek went dry this year, and it is normally a year-round creek. It flowed all last summer, but it's drier than "'dem dry bones" now. Our weeds have done marvelously well!

The timer just went off, so I have to go check on Clementine. I put her on a long lead out back by the blackberry bushes, during the morning, but I try to move her back to her pen by lunchtime because the sun starts getting to that area. She has a nice, shady pen, but she gets tired of being penned up. Goats are great escape artists, and she got loose a couple of weeks ago. She made it all the way to our driveway gate which was fortunately, closed. Schatze, in her living room chair by the window, spotted Clementine and started barking. Since barking in the house is a no-no, I figured I should check it out.

I stepped out the front door and yelled, "Here, Clementine, come on, baby, come see Mama," and clapped my hands. Clementine turned back from the gate, put her tail in the air and stampeded to me as fast as she could run. She won't come to Harry, but I don't have any problem catching her.

Same things with my cats. If I want them to come in from wherever they might be hunting, I just ring a little dinner bell, and they come running. I hope to get some chickens and guineas someday soon, and I plan on training them the same way, especially the guineas, because they are free-range. I'll turn them loose in the morning and call them back in where they will be safe, at night. Training them is a heck of a lot easier than chasing them!

As for the heart problems, I still have arrhythmia and probably always will unless a lot of people start praying for my healing. One of the women in our church had arrhythmia. A lot of people were praying for her, and God healed her. Healing, like a good rainy season this winter and a good snow pack, needs some prayer warriors, praying in faith. People don't seem to want to do that anymore. We've gotten too far away from the Source.

Harry was going to ask the blessing recently, and I said, "What we need to do is pray for rain," so, at the end of his prayer, he asked for rain. As soon as he said "Amen," he followed it with, "We aren't going to get any rain." Well, duh! Of course we won't! If you ask for something and you don't believe it, even as you are asking, you definitely will *not* get it. The Bible says, "If you ask any thing, *believing.* . . ." The problem is, most people have no faith in God's ability to do what He says.

Well, the buzzer went off on the dryer, so I'd better get back to work. It's bad enough having a nagging husband without having nagging appliances. There *ain't* no justice!

Tuesday, August 14, 2001

I got a call last night about 9:30 p.m. from Harry's car-pool partner, telling me that Harry had gone on a "field trip" and should be home today or tomorrow. The company he works for sent him to Alturas, California, where they are fighting fires, to replace a main gear box on one of the helicopters. Alturas is in the northeast corner of California, and I guess they are having a major fire there. We've got a pretty good fire going down by Ashland, which is south-central Oregon, so I guess things are pretty smokey along the California-Oregon border. Harry didn't have any advanced notice, so he didn't even have a change of clothes or a toothbrush. From now on, I think he needs to keep a "ditty bag" at work with toothbrush, razor, clean underwear, change of clothes, etc., because when a helicopter is down, they need someone to go *right now!* I wish everyone would get together and *pray for rain.* It would certainly solve a lot of fire problems.

Wednesday, August 15, 2001

Harry called around 8:30 p.m. "I'm back at Erickson and need a ride home. My car is parked at Wal-Mart in Grants Pass."

I laughed. "I'd say you've got a problem!"

Harry started laughing, "Ooohh-kay."

"I'll bet you're really smelly."

Still laughing, he answered, "Yeah."

"Okay, you can sit in the back of the truck."

Schatze and I drove to Central point to pick him up. Wouldn't you know? I forgot to lock the passenger door, and he got in the front of the truck. Darn! It wasn't so bad for me because I held my nose all the way home, but poor little Schatze was trapped in the back seat with no defense. She coughed, wheezed and pawed at her nose all the way home, much the way a dog does when sprayed by a skunk. She may never recover! All right, all right! So I embellished the facts a little bit. Maybe it wasn't *quite* that bad, but you have to admit it makes a better story than just saying, "Schatze and I picked up Harry and brought him home." Now wasn't that boring?

Thursday, August 16, 2001

We went to the Josephine County Fair this morning. I like County Fairs, and they are about all I have the strength to do anymore. I sure couldn't last through a State Fair!

We saw all the goats, pigs, cattle, chickens, ducks, geese, rabbits and even one guinea, and watched young teens showing their dogs, which was a real hoot! One little girl had a Boxer, and every time she tried to make him stand and place his feet in the proper position, he sat down. In desperation, she grabbed him by his stub of a tail, which looked like and worked well as a handle, and held up his back end. Between holding up his rear end and wiping the slobbers off his face, she really had her hands full. He must have been a really good-natured dog because whatever she did to him, didn't seem to bother him.

Monday, August 20, 2001

Last night, Harry and I took Clementine to Sam's Valley, and the lady from whom I purchased Clementine, clipped her hooves and gave her two shots. I'll probably do both those jobs from now on, if I can purchase the shots.

I had a big (plastic) dog house I wasn't using, and I took the top half off, turned the bottom half upside-down, and placed it in Clementine's pen so she would have something she could jump up on. I noticed that the structure was moved from place to place, and I thought Harry had been moving it. But, Saturday night while I was sitting in the swing on the deck, talking to a friend, I watched Clementine get down on her knees and crawl inside the upended dog house. Then she stood up, lifting it on her back, turned around and moved it over by the fence. She crawled back out, got on top and stood on her hind legs, and she could just reach some of the blackberries that were hanging over the fence. Pretty smart little goat!

Saturday, I went to a Farmer's Market in downtown Grants Pass and bought some organically grown cucumbers. I've been up since 6:30 this morning canning 16 quarts of dill pickles. When we remodeled the kitchen, I bought a ceramic cooktop, not being aware that you can't can (in a pressure canner) on it. It has been a real hassle trying to get the pickles canned, so I'm going to try to sell the ceramic cooktop and get a plain burner cooktop. I told Harry what I really need for canning is an old wood cook stove. (Outside, of course!) Boy, would that heat up the house.

Well, it has cooled down a little bit the last few days, and Harry said we are supposed to get some rain on Wednesday. I sure hope so. Maybe my prayers are going to soon be answered.

Harry is building a handicapped ramp off our front porch, and we're both looking forward to using it. We belong to the Rice Crispies Club. When we move, everything goes snap, crackle, pop! The ramp will be a lot easier than going up and down 5 steps, twenty times a day. Now, maybe we can get a couple of wheel chairs and drag-race down the ramp. Bet I'll win!!

Do you read Ann Landers? Recently, a woman wrote in that her five-year-old started asking for details about sex. When subtle evasion didn't work, and he wanted to know how the seed got into the mommy, she finally agreed to tell him, providing he would not discuss it with other children. When she finished her explanation, he looked towards heaven and exclaimed, "Oh, God, isn't there any other way?" My sentiments, exactly!

A Sunday school teacher was teaching her young students a song, "Oh, the Consecrated Cross I Bear." One of the mothers called and wanted to know what was being taught in that Sunday school class. Her son came home singing, "Oh, the constipated cross-eyed bear."

Guess I'd better close and get back to work. No rest for the weary. No rest for the wicked, either. Makes me wonder which group I'd fall into. No comments, please.

Love and prayers, as always,

Shirlene and Harry

Monday, August 27, 2001

Dear Friends and Family,

He stood about 25 feet away from me in the early evening twilight, watching me water the pussy willow tree that stands above our dry creek bed. Finally, I glanced up and returned his curious gaze—a yearling with two little stubby horns as proof of his male status.

"Well, hello. I'll bet you're back to eat some more of my garden." He listened and continued to watch me but didn't move.

"Shoo, go find something else to eat." I took a few steps toward him and he turned and trotted off a few feet, but didn't leave. Then, he turned sideways, and I got a good look at him. I could almost count the ribs on his small, thin frame, and I realized just how bad the drought has been on the wildlife. There is no food in the woods, not even at the higher elevations, so the deer and other wildlife are coming to the valley in search of food.

Last summer, I came home from a trip to Sacramento, pulled into the drive and parked overlooking the back lawn. When I got out of the pickup, I glanced toward the (then) running creek and was surprised to see a doe and fawn grazing on the lawn. They stared at me for a few minutes, then the doe gave a signal, and they splashed their way up the creek and out of sight. Deer will return, year after year, to the same area, and I am reasonably sure this yearling buck is that little fawn that the mother brought here last year.

I backed away from the small deer, circled the yard and got some alfalfa hay from the RV- storage area. I know, I know! If I feed him, he'll never go away, but I can't stand to see him starve. I made a wide circle around the little buck and put the hay out by the creek. It has been several days now and he either hasn't found the hay, or has decided my garden is much better fare.

My first indication of this little raider was when I noticed my dwarf fruit trees had been stripped of all their leaves. Then, my kale plants had only stems and no tops. I thought Harry might have cut off the tops for a salad mixture, but when I asked him, he said no. I noticed some of my green tomatoes were on the ground. *Hmm, wonder what's causing my tomatoes to fall off the vine while they're still green?* That's when I spotted the small hoof print in the mud, and I knew they had a little help in 'falling.' Upon closer examination, I discovered some of the tomatoes had the tops nipped off. So be it! We wouldn't eat all of it anyway.

I tied some of the tomato plants up off the ground with green plant tape. The next morning the tape was on the ground, and so were the tomato vines. I was disappointed that the tape had come untied—until I spotted the tattletale, hoof print in the mud. Buck (yes, I've named him) had evidently decided to try this new green item, and when he pulled on it, it came untied.

Last summer, after we moved in, I was on the porch one night around 11:00 or 12:00 p.m., and I heard a cougar scream. It was off in the distance, but it still brought a chill up my spine. We *do* live in the mountains.

I had been locking the goat in the shed at night and the cats in the garage, and Harry was ridiculing me for locking them up. "Why do you lock them up? It isn't necessary."

"I lock them up so they'll be safe from predators."

A derogatory snort followed that remark. "We don't have any predators here."

Recently, one of the men Harry rides to work with, who lives about a mile or so up the road from us, told Harry about a cougar that was in his yard, so Harry said, "Maybe you should go ahead and lock the animals up at night."

If a *man* says there are predators, then it must be true, but if a woman—especially a *wife*—says it, it is just nonsense. Men automatically figure their wives don't know what they are talking about. A woman can be the most brilliant, intelligent woman in the world while she is dating a man, but the minute she marries him, she becomes (in his eyes) somebody who doesn't know anything. I finally figured out why this is true. It's because she was dumb enough to marry him! He knows himself very well, and he figures if she were really bright, she wouldn't have married him. Probably a lot of truth in that!

A husband and wife took the grandkids to a cabin by the lake for the weekend. The husband got into his boat, went out on the lake and fished while his wife watched the rambunctious grandkids. When he finally returned, she wanted some peace and quiet to read her book, so she left him with the grandkids, got into his boat and rowed to a quiet spot to read. A game warden's boat cruised near her and stopped. "What are you doing here?" he asked.

"I thought it was obvious. I'm reading."

"Well, you are in a restricted fishing area, so I'll have to give you a ticket."

"But I'm not fishing, I'm reading."

"Yes, but you've got all the right equipment with you."

"Well, then, I'll have to charge you with rape."

"Lady, I haven't touched you!"

"I know, but you've got all the right equipment."

Moral of the story: Be cautious around women who read; they may also be capable of thinking. The little 'story' is one I read (someplace?), but the moral of the story is mine!

Wednesday, August 29, 2001

Last night I finished watering and took care of the animals while a three-quarter, pot-bellied moon hung just off the third star to the left. Dark comes early and more quickly now, and old Mother Earth is warning of an early fall. Leaves are already floating silently down and will soon blanket the back yard. The mustard greens and parsley are getting ready to drop their seeds, and a gentle breeze is waiting to scatter them. One season soon to exit and another waiting in the wings, ready to enter.

As I was locking up the animals for the night, I noticed a rather long "worm" in the driveway. On closer examination, the worm turned out to be a (dead) baby snake, about eight inches long. I don't know if my Manx cats killed him or if he was in the wrong place at the right time, and Harry ran over him. His head was missing, but the rest of him wasn't mashed flat, so I think, maybe, the cats got him. Manx are pretty good snake patrollers. That's the only snake I have seen this summer, and it wouldn't have hurt my feelings if I hadn't seen him. I enjoy most of the animal life we have, living here in the mountains, but that is one segment I could gladly do without.

We're still having hot weather here, but now in the nineties instead of 100's, and the evenings are cooler. The ground isn't drying out as fast, and the plants aren't taking as much water, so now I am able to finish and sit on the back deck in the porch swing for fifteen or twenty minutes each evening while the cooling breeze caresses plants, animals and yours truly. What a nice way to unwind after a hectic day of activity. Wish I had time to do more sitting and swinging. Ah, well.

Harry is still working on the handicapped ramp, and it is slowly taking shape. We have five steps going from the front porch to the ground, so going down and back up is ten steps, and I figured that I make at least 15 trips a day, sometimes more, up and down those steps, so that is an average of 150 up/down steps a day! No wonder my muscles ache when I go to bed at night. It will be so nice to have the ramp finished.

Labor Day is almost here, but that's no big deal at this place. *Every day* is a labor day! We never seem to catch up. Mowing, weeding, planting, weeding, pruning, weeding, watering and fertilizing, so we can do more weeding. There's a moral in there someplace. I've named this property *The Garden of Weedin'.*

Harry said, "Monday is Labor Day, and I don't have to work." I laughed. And laughed! "Oh, yes you do. You're just not going to get paid for it." Silly man!

I finally found a young boy, seventeen-years-old, who wants to work. Most of the kids I tried to hire don't show up, or if they do, they don't want to work after they get here. They want the pay, they just don't want the work. This young man, Raymond, shows up on time, works without my standing over him, does a good job, and wonder of wonders, knows the difference between a weed and a flower! I'm going to have him teach Harry! Harry pulls my flowers and carefully pats the dirt around the weeds!! I suspect he does it on purpose, so I won't ask him to do the weeding. Anyway, Raymond is working for me now, one day a week, and my flower beds actually *look* like flower beds. Before Raymond worked on them, they looked like an experiment in growing weed patches, with a couple of flowers thrown in.

One of the magazines I have subscribed to for years, *Organic Gardening*, has *reorganized*, and they are now OG— with a higher price, of course. The magazine is supposed to be about an organic "lifestyle," and they have full-page ads on drugs. Hello? The magazine is 49 pages (counting the inside back cover), and 17 ½ of those pages are ads! They asked for comments on their "new" magazine (a big mistake on their part) and boy, did I give 'em comments! I'll bet my Aunt Aggie's underdrawers they won't ask again!

Well, folks, my desk is piled high with junk that I need to sort through, shred, throw away, file or otherwise deal with. I have been working on the theory of "ignore it, and it will go away." I figured if I procrastinated long enough, it would just disappear. It didn't. (Sigh!) Guess there is no choice, so I'd better quit gabbing and get to work. My love and prayers,

Shirlene & Harry

September 16, 2001

Dear Friends and Family,

Yesterday, we had a little rain. Not much, but it was better than nothing, and last night, we had some high fog that rolled in and dampened the ground. It didn't last long, but between the small amount of rain and fog, I walked the yard this morning on dew-kissed grass. Nice.

While I was circling the back yard, getting in my morning walk, a solitary goose flew over, frantically calling out, trying to locate the flock. It is rare to see one solitary goose. I don't know how he got separated from the group, but his lonely cries echoed his panic as he disappeared into the high fog.

The melody of the wind changes with the seasons, and the breeze has been whispering that summer is on the way out, and fall is entering from off stage. In the summer the wind floats through the leaves as silently and gently as a deer, and in the fall, it rustles the leaves like a lonely coyote's cry. When winter arrives and there is nothing to impede its progress, it howls through the branches like a wolf on the prowl. Listen, and Mother Earth will sing you her own serenade.

The handicapped ramp is finished and really looks nice. It is certainly easier on the knees and hips than going up and down steps. We also have two, new, two-foot by two-foot sky lights in the den area, and wonder of wonders, the dirt is finally going back into the garden pit. There is some hope that it may be finished before winter sets in, so it will be ready for next spring.

I bought cinder block to replace the rotted-out wood that surrounded the small planter bed of tomatoes in the back yard. Harry got the blocks in place, and I'm sure the deer appreciated his efforts because they were all over the tomatoes last night, and into the second planter bed where I have planted a few winter vegetables.

A couple of days ago, Harry knocked on the window and said, "The deer are in the back yard." I went out on the porch and Buck, our yearling, was lying down in the shade at the back, by the creek, and a new fawn with almost-faded spots was lying a short distance away. Unusual to see a fawn with a yearling buck, but I suspect the mother may have been killed. They both looked at us while we went on about our business, and about ten minutes later, they ambled down into the dry creek and disappeared.

I usually get up during the night and let Schatze out to do her business, and every now and then, we startle something that is wandering through our yard, looking for food. About a week ago, Schatze went to her potty area, did her business and started back toward the house. Then she stopped and peered into the darkness. I looked that direction, and a large doe stood still as a stone, in the middle of the back yard by our old, dead stump. Because she was so still, Schatze couldn't figure out if it was something alive, so she headed back to the house. Then she stopped, went again to the edge of the back driveway and looked into the dark. The deer never moved a muscle. She looked like one of those large, lawn statues. Schatze repeated the process one more time, only this time, she finally decided there actually was something out there that was obviously much bigger than she is, so she made a very hasty dash to the safety of the house. My brave guard dog!

Several nights ago, I let Schatze out around 4:30 a.m., and she bailed off the end of the ramp on the run, growling all the way. This was something more her size, but much more dangerous. She was after a racoon, that appeared to be about her size, possibly a little larger. I yelled for her to come back, which she ignored, but fortunately, the racoon got up the tree and out of the way. If she'd caught it, it probably would have severely injured or perhaps killed her. Racoons have been known to kill dogs several times larger than themselves. Somehow, I need to get a message to this goofy little dog that deer are okay to chase—they will run—but racoons are dangerous and best left alone.

The newscaster said Osama bin Laden was thanking "God" for all the Americans he had killed, and it really aggravated me that the media was using the term "God." If people hear a Muslim say, "Praise Allah," they think it means God. Muslims do not worship the God of the Bible. The sign on the Muslim temple is a crescent moon, which represents Allah, the Moon God, which originated from pagan idolatry. It has nothing to do with the one true God of the Bible. We have gotten so far away from God's word, the majority of this nation doesn't know the difference.

From the beginning of man's entry into this world, God has protected *His* people as long as they stayed with Him and worshiped Him. But, throughout time, people have wandered away from God and gone their own way. When that happens, God backs off and lets them be conquered and ruled by idolatrous nations. Only when they repent and return to God will He hear their prayers. The key word is *repent,* and I wonder if our nation will do that. Thousands are now running to the churches and praying for God to help us, but most people have a concept that God is just sitting up there to be ignored except when we get into trouble. Then, He is supposed to be a puppet God who answers when they jerk the string. Not! It just doesn't work that way.

God's Word, 2 Chronicles 7:14, says: *"IF* my people, *which are called by my name,* (Christians) shall humble themselves and pray, and seek my face, *and turn from their wicked ways;* then will I hear from heaven, and will forgive their sin, and will heal their land." (emphasis, mine.)

October 1, 2001

From the beginning date of this letter, to today's date, I probably don't have to tell you that I got *somewhat* sidetracked. A perpetual state, I think.

I had overnight, out-of-town company last Monday night, and we were sitting here visiting, about dusk, when I looked out the window and spotted the area-resident doe, eating the volunteer cantaloupe that Harry has been protecting. As Carol and I watched, I knocked on the window to frighten the doe away, but she ignored me. I said, "Schatze, you want to go chase the deer?" Of course, she didn't know what I was saying, but she caught the excitement in my voice and began to jump up and down. "Come on," I told her, and raced out the back door. I opened the gate to the pasture and was inside, hurrying up the hill before the deer moved. When the doe moved, Schatze spotted her and gave a rr-ruf, ruff, chase. The deer bomp, bomp, boi-oi-nged over the fence to safety, while Schatze ran around the pasture in a fourteen-pound frenzy of excited triumph, rr-ruf, rr-ruffing every few seconds to let me know what a good job she did of getting rid of that big monster.

Carol had watched the action out the dining room window, and when we came back into the house, she and I were laughing at Schatze's victory. I asked Schatze, "Did you get that deer?" and she raced around the living room, around the dining room table, down the hallway and into my bedroom, then back into the living room, four or five times. Each time she hit the living room area, she barked to show us how she had chased and gotten rid of the deer. She kept Carol and me laughing for several minutes. She was so proud of herself!

I found two, dead snakes in the driveway, each about twelve-to-fourteen inches long. I put one in a container to take to the OSU Master Gardener's clinic for identification, but when I got there, they didn't have any books on snakes, so I went to the local library and finally found one that fit the description. It turned out they were harmless, colorful little garter snakes, with a coral stripe down the center of their back, bordered on each side by black stripes and then yellow. I'll leave them alone if they'll leave me alone. I can't give that guarantee for the cats!

The day Carol arrived, as we were bringing her travel items up the ramp, I noticed Mischief pawing at my *Pieris Japonica* plant. I looked to see what she was after. . . a little snake! As Carol and I watched, Mischief grabbed the snake, threw it up in the air and then pounced on it. After slightly injuring the snake, she turned it loose and backed off. *"Okay, snake, go for it, and see if you can get away before I catch you."* We left her playing her game. Even though the snake was harmless, if I'd been in the flower bed and gotten that snake on me, I'd have probably had to come in the house and change my clothes!

How's that for welcoming company to your house? Show them the snakes in your flower beds! Welcome to life in the country!

Nights are cool here now, down around forty degrees, and sometimes, there is dew on the grass when I get up in the mornings. I am keeping pretty close track of the night-time temperatures, because soon I will have to bring in my lemon and orange trees, my geraniums and petunias. The days are still pretty warm, eighty to ninety-something degrees, so I'm hoping some of my tomatoes will still ripen before a frost hits. I have four tomatoes in containers that I plan on bringing inside, but I don't know if they will produce. Wish I had a greenhouse. I have the glass for it, but not the remainder of the materials. Ah, well, maybe next year.

The freezer and pantry are well stocked, so I guess we are fairly well prepared for winter, except for getting our wood for the stove. Wood is high, but it is cheaper than the utility costs, and a lot warmer.

Well, enough for this session. As usual, the work is waiting for me to get off my 'can' and get busy. The "ignore it, and it will go away" theory just isn't working! My love and prayers,

Shirlene and Harry

October 2, 2001

Dear Friends and Family,

Take an ounce of sunset, a cup of harvest moon, two ounces of silver-pink clouds, a pinch of coolness, the song of crickets and the sighing of trees. Mix with the fresh fragrance of pine needles, cedar trees, crunchy leaves and chrysanthemums. Pour into a gentle, laid-back breeze that washes your face like a touch of silk, and you have Essence of Fall.

What a lovely time of year. A time to pause, to stop and smell the fragrance of another season, to sit on the back porch swing and watch the geese honk their way across the sky. Summer vegetables are going to seed, trees are dropping leaves, and Mother Earth is sighing, getting ready for a long, winter rest. It is a time of reflection, a time of slowing down, and I, too, am ready for a rest.

It has been a busy, frantic summer, and I am not sorry to see it end. It isn't that I won't be busy, but it will be a different kind of busy. A much-needed, very welcome, change of pace. *Inside* things, that have been put on the back burner of summer procrastination, may eventually get done. I hope!

October 10, 2001

I didn't get very far with this letter, so I'll try again. I managed to save the tulips I planted last year because they were in containers, but the gophers (or something) got my daffodils. I bought some more for next Spring, and I'm planting them in containers. Couldn't someone please invent a "gopher bomb?"

The wire is on the sides and top of the fifteen-by-twenty foot garden area, and the gates are being made, so we will soon have an enclosed garden area. Ha, Ha, Ha, gophers, deer, racoons, possums, skunks and miscellaneous critters. No more free restaurant!

We had another nocturnal visitor a couple of nights ago. Whatever it was, tipped over the dog food barrel, but the lid stayed locked on, so it didn't get any food. The culprit was evidently working on getting the barrel open when I let Schatze out just before 6:00 a.m. for her morning constitutional. She shot off the end of the handicapped ramp like a rocket and chased "something" up a tree, but it was still too dark to see what it was. By a process of elimination, I am pretty sure it was a racoon. I'm sure it wasn't a possum because they can't move all that fast, and it would have 'sulled-up.' Thank God, it wasn't a skunk!

We've had several days of clouds that promised rain and didn't produce, but tonight we have a light rain falling. A couple of nights of light frosts finished off the tomato vines. Zap! Dead and black. I have lots of green tomatoes, yet to be picked. I managed to get my geraniums and petunias, and my lemon and orange trees brought in before the frost got them, so I now have a plant jungle just inside the front door. I expect to see monkeys swinging through the area, any day now, and hear Harry give out a Tarzan yell. (He's been waiting for an excuse.)

My friend, Carol, from Sacramento, visited a couple of days this week, and I am expecting other out-of-state company in the next week or two. The geese are flying south and the visitors are migrating north. That's a nice exchange! Friends and family are more interesting companions than geese.

Carol and I toured Old Town in Grants Pass, had a soda at the old-fashioned soda fountain in the Grants Pass Pharmacy, and then drove to Galice to have lunch. Galice, as I think I mentioned in a previous letter, is a sum-total of *one* building, but to make sure you don't miss it, it has a sign that says, "This is Galice." They serve lunch on the back deck, and you sit on picnic benches that are harder than rocks, but Carol and I outfoxed them. I had a couple of pillows in the pickup, and we sat on soft pillows like a couple of queens on a throne. The wasps have retired for the summer, the air was pleasantly cool and crisp, but warm enough to be comfortable, and the river below flowed uncluttered with the usual summer river rafters. There were only two other families on the deck, so we pretty much had the place to ourselves. A nice fall outing.

October 12, 2001

Wednesday night's rain wasn't the heavy, ground-soaking kind, but it did help. It took two days for the rain to get down from the mountains, but our creek has water in it again. Yea! Not the flow we previously had, and not enough yet to clean out all the leaves that have covered it, but water in the bottom and a soft trickle. If we get a couple more rains, it will be flowing again. A nice promise.

Late this afternoon, I re-potted a couple of house plants and cleaned out the goat shed. What a mess Clementine makes! I cleaned up all the droppings and old straw, put in new sawdust shavings and fresh straw and then got a sharp chest pain and had to stop. Harry came out back, so I asked him to put the old straw in the tractor wagon, and I hauled it to the garden area where he dumped and raked it. Our garden composting has begun! We are also burying our kitchen garbage in the garden area. Hopefully, by spring, we should have a good portion of the garden soil composted and ready to plant.

I picked tomatoes last night and have four good-sized containers of green tomatoes. We could have a Fried Green Tomato Fest for the town of Merlin. Hopefully, next year, I'll get them planted sooner and have ripe tomatoes, instead of green. Even getting them planted late, enough ripened to keep us in fresh tomatoes most of the summer, but if all these green ones had ripened, I would have had enough to can.

Thank the good Lord I have two computers! My big computer has been down for over a week, which means I haven't been able to use my printer. I usually do my writing on the laptop, save on an A-drive disc and then print off the big, computer printer. I've been using Harry's printer, but the menus are different, and it is like going into foreign territory.

Harry is trying to correct the problem with mine, so maybe I'll be back in business soon.

Statistics relate that last year, over twenty-three million American Families paid a lot of money for things that looked funny and didn't work. Three million of those were antiques, the rest were college students!

A clever, shoe-shine boy put up a sign, "Left Shoe Shined Free."

And a sign in an office reads, "The easiest way to make ends meet is to get off your own." I especially like that one.

October 16, 2001

Si-I-I-I-I-gh! With all the interruptions, I can't seem to get a letter finished in one sitting, so I'll give it another try.

The front lawn was covered with a flock of about thirty robins early this evening, and Schatze was on her chair at the living room window, growling, letting them know they were in her territory. They can't hear her, of course, but she doesn't know that, so she's happy that she's done her duty. With the weather changing and rain expected, the birds are trying to find food before the rain comes. A big gust of wind whipped through here, scattering leaves everywhere, and the robins scattered with the wind.

I usually feed the goat and cats and lock them up around 7:00 p.m., just as it is getting dark, but tonight, with clouds rolling in, it was getting dark earlier and the cats were on the front porch, meowing to be fed, so I fed and locked up Clementine and both cats at 6:30 . The birds are no longer on the lawn and have flown off to find shelter. It is not quite seven o'clock, and it is very dark, with the inky darkness that comes from a sky blotted out by black clouds. Trees are swaying and branches are swishing around the trees like full skirts on a dancing lady. The rain is coming, and the animals are always the first to know.

We bought a load of firewood this past week and scouted the town for loading-pallets to stack the wood on, so it won't be on the wet ground. We have a small-roofed area on the south side of the garage, and Harry made a pallet floor, under the covered area. The ends and back section next to the fence are still open, but Harry suggested we get siding to match the garage and enclose those areas. Then, we'd have a fairly dry, wood area. Another project! We also need to build a wood box, and I suggested an outside box with a door cut into the wall. That way, we can keep most of the wood mess out of the living room. Yet, *another* project.

When I get up in the morning, I fix tea and toast, bring it into the living room and eat it while I read my morning devotionals. One morning recently, I got interrupted and had to leave the room. When I came back, my dish was sitting on the footstool, but the toast wasn't on it. Aloud, I wondered, "What did I do with that toast?" At precisely that point, Schatze gave out a loud bu-u-r-r-r-p. Mystery solved. She is the only dog I've ever been around that burps after she eats. I said, "Schatze, did you get my toast?!" and she tucked her tail, ran to her bed in the dog carrier and hid. I'm surprised she didn't drink the tea.

When I brought my plants in from outside, I inadvertently brought in a "critter." A small frog was in one of the tomato plants I tried to save, and, after getting into the house, he abandoned the tomato plant for more interesting terrain. For a couple of nights, I heard him "chip, chip, chirrup," but Schatze and I couldn't find him. Then, a couple of nights ago while Harry and I were sitting in the living room reading, the frog decided to go exploring and came hopping across the living room carpet. (Harry wasn't aware of his residency until that moment. . . I figured no sense frightening him.) The little frog, about the size of a quarter, hippity, hopped across the rug. I said, "Harry, can you catch him?"

"Yes," he assured me, and the race was on. Harry was on his hands and knees on the carpet, hopping around behind the escapee, trying to cup his hand over the frog, who was desperately trying to flee from the monster, to a safety area under the sofa. I gave moral support by sitting in my chair, laughing like crazy and yelling, "Get him, Harry." A real Keystone Cops episode. The best entertainment I've had in ages! Who needs TV? The frog was finally caught and released outside in the flower beds. Our own, personal, Catch and Release program.

A kindergarten class visited a farm, and one of the boys was later asked to describe how to milk a cow. "Well," he replied, "you sit on a stool next to the cow, and then you grab the gutters."

My love and prayers until next time.

Shirlene and Harry

October 23, 2001

Dear Friends and Family,

    Yesterday was the first real rain of the season and the first fire in the wood stove. It wasn't all that cold—around fifty degrees—so I lit the fire just before going to bed, to take the chill off, but didn't keep it going all night. The house was still cozy and warm when we got up this morning. A few after-thought showers trailed at the end of the clouds today, but the sun has been out much of the day, and the grass is bathed and cleaned, like a child spiffied-up for Sunday school.

Boy, I'll bet that 'spiffied-up' phrase is going to give my spell-checker fits! Every time I use some colloquialism or off-the-wall word, the spell checker comes up with some really weird suggestions (like telling me where to go!). It's a good thing the spell checker can't talk.

I went to the Planning Commission Office to get building permits for our chicken house. The lady started pulling out big ledgers, and spieling off what kind and how many building permits I have to have. "It has to be at least thirty-five feet from your neighbor's property line."

The creek is in the back, on the west side, so my neighbors on that side are across the creek and up the bank, and there is only a pasture and an old gnarled apple orchard full of overgrown blackberries and teasel in back of the pasture, on the north side. When I explained that, she said, "Yes, but that might change, and it might later be inhabited." I refrained from telling her that it already is. . . several deer live there, along with mice, rabbits, gophers (although most of those live in MY yard,) ticks, and snakes. "If you build anything over eighteen inches high," she continued, "you have to have a development permit."

I laughed. "Eighteen inches?!"

The man at the counter next to me quipped, "Buildings for the 'Little People.' "

"Well, I'm Irish," I laughed. "I believe in the 'Little People'."

She went on to explain more rules and regulations, and I finally collapsed on the counter, laughing. "Ma'am," I told her, "I'm just going to build a chicken coop, not Buckingham Palace." (If I start raising ducks, I could call it Duckingham Palace.)

She looked a little embarrassed, but was laughing with me. "I know. It's ridiculous, isn't it?"

"Yes." It was the first thing we'd agreed on!

If we don't get too bogged down in bureaucratic, red tape, we hope to get the chicken pen and goat pen built, or at least started, within the next month. But, it sounds like it might take six months just to get the permits. Are we having fun, yet?

The racoons have figured out how to get the lid off the cat food barrel, and they've been in the barrel helping themselves and generally making a mess. I tied the lid on with a bungee cord, and they figured out how to get that off, so I finally had to move both the cat and dog food barrels into the garage.

My cats were yowling and screeching this morning, so I opened the door to see what was outside. Schatze went out with me, and we discovered a big black cat from the other side of the creek, exploring our yard. Schatze bailed off the end of the ramp, ready for a chase, but instead of running, the cat turned and faced her, back arched and claws ready. Schatze came to a screeching halt, looked warily at the cat, decided she didn't want her nose scratched, and turned and came back to the porch. She's willing to give chase as long as they turn and run, but when they stop to fight, the fun goes out of the game. One of my cats, Mischief, knows this and refuses to run, but C.C. has never caught on and has become an unwilling partner in the game of chase.

October 30, 2001

I went out back to inspect the creek and found it flowing again, although still low and not enough water to clean out all the summer debris.

The rain drizzled softly, off and on, until about 2:00 a.m., then got down to business and rained until after 9:00 this morning. We must have gotten a substantial amount in the surrounding mountains for the creek to now be running so well. I love it! This poor, dry earth is absorbing the water like a sponge.

November 9, 2001

No, I didn't go on an Arctic expedition, I've just had company for a couple of weeks and haven't been able to finish this letter. The guests had a small Schnauzer and Schatze took one look at her and decided she had a playmate. Problem is, Muff is ten years old and not in any mood to put up with nonsense from this two-year-old puppy. Schatze bounced all around Muff, spoi-oi-ng, spoi-oi-ng, spoing, then rolled over in front of her, but Muff just growled a warning and stomped off in stiff-legged indignation. *Stupid puppy, I don't want to play!* However, Schatze doesn't give up easily. She soon discovered Muff doesn't want to be touched, so she would run by Muff and touch her or bump into her. Muff would whirl around, growling and snapping and give chase, while Schatze gleefully ran circles around her, challenging, *C'mon, c'mon, catch me if you can!*

Muff had several of her toys on the floor, and Schatze grabbed one, took it to the back of her bed and hid it. Muff grabbed the other one and went into the next room with it, growling a warning at Schatze with every step. Schatze decided not to pursue the matter, and turned and walked away. Muff immediately turned around, followed Schatze and laid the toy on the floor between them. *Go ahead, see if you can get it.* The game was on. They have provided endless entertainment!

Guess what I discovered? They DO make a gopher bomb! Actually, it is a small 'stick' about six inches long that you put in the gopher hole, and it gases them to death (hopefully). I'm not so sure it will work with my gophers because they seem to be well versed in human vs. gopher warfare. All of my gophers probably have gas masks! If I could just figure out how to catch all the gophers and racoons, I could ship 'em out to all of you lovely people as Christmas presents. Or probably put a sign out by the road and pass them off as pets. Glue some long hair on the gophers and pass them off as Guinea Pigs, and possibly pass the racoons off as ring-tailed Mambusu cats. People will buy *anything* at Christmas time! (In case you're wondering what a Mambusu Cat is. . . I haven't the foggiest, I just made that up!)

I went into the garage tonight and saw a really big, ugly bug on the floor, so I stepped on him before he could find a mate and create a multitude of little ugly bugs. He was probably on his way to the Ugly Bug Ball, but I guarantee, I put a crimp in his tuxedo. Tomorrow, I'll get out the bug book and see if I can find out what he was. Wish I had a good microscope, so I could really examine some of these homely creatures. Many of them look like they were put together by a committee of frantic, frustrated engineers, or Kindergartners with left-over tinker toys and glue.

Tomorrow morning, early (ugh), we have to go to the Sanitary Land Fill with a load of trash. It beats the heck out of me why they call something as gross as a garbage dump, a "Sanitary" *anything*, because it is anything *but* sanitary! Go figure! We've been here a year and a half (almost), and we're still trying to clean up the trash the previous tenants left. Today, we found another old tire, and I've lost count on how many that makes. They must have had a used tire lot here.

At some point in time, someone put a new roof on this place, and they threw all the old roofing shingles out back and let the blackberries grow over them, along with the tires, old wire and other garbage. Why couldn't they have hidden something useful, like money, gold or other buried treasure? I tell you, there *ain't* no justice!

An acquaintance left two cats here for me to "cat-sit" while she gets moved and settled, so I now have my two cats and two visitors. This place is turning into a regular cat-house!

Remarks like that make Harry's face turn red so I manage to say enough off-the-wall things to keep him red-faced and running. (It doesn't take much!) Two or three red faces and Harry runs for the outside. He says he's going out to work, but *I know* he's escaping.

November 22, 2001

Happy Thanksgiving! We went out to dinner at noon, but other than that, have spent the day quietly, resting and watching the rain. The ground is thoroughly saturated and squishes when you walk on it. The sun came out for a short time and skipped sunbeams across the puddles in the drive, and the fog (or clouds) settled into the crevices of the mountains like filling in a jelly roll. Clementine, our goat, hates the rain and stays in her shed, occasionally sticking her head out the door and bleating her indignation and protest.

We've had almost a full week of good, steady rain and the creek has more water in it now than at any time since we moved in. It's flowing full and swift and you can hear it rushing over the rocks, all the way from the yard next to the house, over 100 feet from the stream.

I can't believe it has taken me so long to get back to this, but everything has happened. My company was here for two weeks and two days, and the last three or four days they were here, I was in total pain. I managed to injure the trapezius muscle in my right shoulder, and it affected my neck, right arm, and it even hurt to chew food. On the fifth day with no relief from the pain, I finally went to a clinic, found out what was wrong, and got some medicine. The medicine made me sleepy, so, for the next three days, I didn't feel like doing anything, and slept about ten hours each night. It must have been good for me, because it finally cleared up.

After the company left with their little dog, Schatze was so lonely she just wandered around the house and searched for Muff. Coincidentally, on the day they left, I was in contact with a woman who was trying to find a home for a little Jack Russell Terrier. She brought the dog by the house to meet us, and the Terrier and Schatze became instant buddies. The woman checked out several homes that day, then called me the next day and said she felt the dog would have the best home with me. We now have a one-year-old Jack Russell Terrier named Trudy, and Schatze is in seventh heaven. She finally has a play buddy.

Trudy is built slender with long legs, like a Greyhound, only much smaller. She and Schatze are almost the exact same height, but Schatze outweighs Trudy. When I take them out in the back yard to play, Trudy chases Schatze, and then they reverse and Schatze chases Trudy. With Trudy's streamlined body and long legs, she's built for speed. Schatze is fast, but she can't outrun Trudy, and it really makes her frustrated when she can't catch her. When they stop for a moment, Schatze is panting for breath, and Trudy isn't even breathing hard. They chase, romp, roll, play tug-of-war with the toys, and provide endless hours of entertainment.

I can't believe that December is almost here, and it is time to get out the Christmas decorations. My life is speeding by as swiftly as our fast-flowing creek, but I praise God for each day. Even though we have a war going on, I find so many things for which to be thankful. The health that I have (with all my problems, I see people much worse off than me), family and friends, a roof over my head, food on the table, a good bed to sleep in, a stove for warmth. Too many blessings to list! How truly blessed we are.

I read a couple of jokes someplace (as usual, I can't remember where), and thought they were cute:

Two fellows were discussing an upcoming wedding. "It's a dollar and sense wedding," one said.

"What do you mean?"

"He hasn't got a dollar, and she hasn't any sense."

If you think that one was bad, two farmers were boasting about the strongest wind they'd seen. The first one boasted, "You know those giant redwoods in California? Well, once the wind got so strong, it bent them right over."

"That's nothing," the second farmer said. "On my farm in Kansas, we had a wind that blew a hundred miles an hour. One of my hens had her back to the wind, and she laid the same egg six times."

My dad used to tell that joke, when I was a kid.

Best I close this rambling nonsense. Hope everyone is safe and well.

God keep you in His care.

Shirlene and Harry

November 29, 2001

D ear Friends and Family,

All summer long I prayed for rain, and now, God is answering all those prayers at once. It has rained steadily for almost two weeks, with only a two-day let-up during that time. Today, it hasn't even let up long enough for Schatze and Trudy to go outside. They are both reluctant to go out in the rain, even with coats on, which they both despise. They'd like to play tug-of-war with the coats, so I have to keep them up high, beyond reach. Twice today I've taken the broom and 'swept' both dogs off the porch into the rain, telling them to go potty. I think they'd rather stay in the house and keep their legs crossed! I took them out to the covered parking RV area, where they usually go, and they greeted the cats, sniffed around a bit, stayed under the roof for a few minutes and then made a bee-line for the warm, dry house. Those dogs are no dummies!

The 'girls' grabbed a toy out of the toy box and are playing tug of war. Last night, I had them both in my lap, in the recliner. Harry says, "And they call it a dog's life?" They are so much company, not only for each other, but for me. And, wonder of wonder, even for grumpy old Harry. Trudy has convinced him, twice now, that she should lie across his lap and go to sleep, while he pets and rocks her. This, from a sworn dog-hater! Will miracles never cease?

The creek was running high and muddy, then in the two days without rain, it dropped back almost to normal. When I closed up the animals tonight, I checked on the creek. It is on the rise again, higher, muddier and swifter than before. There is a small island in the middle of the creek that has a crooked tree growing on it. In normal times, the water flows gently around the island. Now, it has covered the island and swirls angrily around the tree. If the rain continues and the creek gets much higher, we will have to find some source of sand bags to keep it out of the yard.

I guess I've become a 'naturalized Oregonian' because I've developed web feet! If the creek keeps rising, I may need them. I keep thinking the rain is going to stop for a few minutes, so I can go get some more wood, but it looks like I'll have to put on my coat and get wet, for there haven't been any signs of stopping. Our little wood stove has certainly provided a nice, warm heat during this rainy period. The dogs take turns snoozing on the rug in front of the hearth, or looking through the glass and watching the flames, which seem to fascinate them.

I think I need a rain suit. I have rubber boots, which are a necessity now, because the goat pen is a muddy mess. I don't have a raincoat or pants, so going out to take care of animals, get wood and check the creek are damp adventures.

Wouldn't you know? As soon as I got the animals all locked up and got back inside, the rain finally stopped, and the clouds that have been dumping barrels of water became fog and settled around the trees in a misty cloak. Night settles in quickly now, almost like someone dropped a curtain, or turned out a light.

Harry took a week of vacation at Thanksgiving, supposedly to get some work done around here, but of course, it rained all week. I'm sure he sneaked around behind my back and prayed extra hard for rain all week long. He has another week of vacation from Christmas through New Year's, and he'll probably pray for more bad weather. He's getting really sneaky in his old age. (He doesn't mind my saying he's getting sneaky, but he resents the "old age" bit.)

When my company was here, I came staggering into the living room, half asleep. They took one look at me and said, "Did you wake up grumpy?"

"No," I told them. "I'm going to let him sleep." It's an old joke, but it was appropriate.

Well, Christmas is just around the corner, so I suppose I'll get out the decorations this weekend and decorate the house. I hope I can locate the Nativity and figurines. I knew where they were, but Harry has moved everything in the garage, and now, nothing makes sense. Boxes of sewing supplies are piled on top of my herb containers, Christmas items are scattered among canning jars and equipment, and garage sale items that *were* sorted and set aside, have been scattered and intermingled among everything. No organization, rhyme or reason, and not much chance of finding whatever you are looking for. When I have to search for something I need, with no chance of finding it, I remind him he should be shot by a firing squad, before breakfast, and without a blindfold! Rolls off his back like water off a duck's back, and with about as much effect.

Christmas will be a quiet affair this year, with just the two of us. If I fix a big dinner, I will do it Christmas Eve day, and we will have warm-ups Christmas day. That allows me to relax and enjoy the day, to read Luke's account of Christ's birth, enjoy some Christmas carols and reflect on the true meaning of the day. I rather like my quiet Christmases.

I may not get another letter written before Christmas, so I want to wish each and every one the blessings of this Holy season. The birth of a Savior! What a joyous message. May the message of His love, grace and forgiveness be with you throughout each day of the coming year, and may you have His peace to lead you through these uncertain days of terrorism.

These things I have spoken unto you, that in me you might have peace. In the world, ye shall have tribulation, but be of good cheer; I have overcome the world. (John 16:33 KJV)

May you have a wonderful, joyous and safe Christmas and New Year, and may you walk through it holding God's hand.

Wishing you a blessed Christmas, from all the gang at our house, to all the gang at yours.

Shirlene, Harry, Schatze, Trudy, Mischief, C.C., Clementine, and our two guest cats.

December 4, 2001

Dear Friends and Family,

The Christmas letter went out the last week of November, and the house was decorated the last day of November, so now I can sit back and enjoy the season, right? Ha! It's a nice thought and to some extent, true. My shopping was done by October, but there are always last minute things to do. I'd really like to do some Christmas baking, but each day seems filled to the brim, and so far, no baking has been started.

My two house mates, Trudy and Schatze, keep me entertained with their antics, and the Grinch, a.k.a., Harry, works hard at filling in with pre-holiday 'grumping.' I actually saw him break forth in a couple of unsolicited smiles, once or twice yesterday! If he's not careful, he could lose his Scrooge image.

After much exploratory surgery and expensive parts, Harry's old 'Lizzy' gave up the ghost and died. I think that car has been running on the power of prayer for the past two or three years, and finally, even God gave up on keeping it running. Yesterday, we went car shopping. Not my favorite thing to do, so I hedged my bets with prayer before we started. I prayed for a nice, clean car in really good condition, in good mechanical shape, low mileage and a good (low) price. Okay, okay, so I asked for a miracle! Well, He *is* God, you know, and everyday miracles are no big deal for Him, so I asked. God never ceases to delight me with His answers.

After looking at a few clunkers that were in worse shape than the deceased one at home, God led us to a 1992 Chevy Caprice, four-door, immaculate inside and beautiful on the outside, excellent mechanical condition and only 75,000 original miles. The owner had been sick for several years with a kidney illness and hadn't driven it a lot before he died this past August. His wife decided to trade in both their vehicles and get herself a four-wheel drive, so she had taken her husband's car to the dealer not long before we got there. They hadn't even had time to finish her paperwork or detail the car, but it was so clean, it didn't need detailed. It is a beautiful, soft rust-red, with a paint sealant that gives it extra shine. We got it for $3,600. Does God answer prayer? You bet'cha!

When they were filling out the paperwork and Harry knew he was getting the car, he tried valiantly to maintain his

'Joe Cool' image, and did, in fact, manage *not* to tap dance across the salesman's desk. However, he couldn't control the Cheshire Cat grins that kept escaping. I'm almost sure when they handed him the keys and the salesman and I turned away, he did a Snoopy dance on the way out to the car.

I have the inside of the house all decorated for Christmas and was hoping to get Harry to hang the outside lights, but I knew my chance of getting that done after the purchase of his car, was absolutely zilch! I was right. After breakfast was over, he spent most of the morning sitting in his car, like King Tut in a new chariot! Well, he didn't spend al-l-l-l of the morning doing that. . . he spent part of it wiping imaginary dirt spots off the exterior. I told him the only difference between him and my five-year-old grandson, Parker, was that Harry's toys cost more. So guess what Harry's Christmas present is this year? Yup!

It has rained almost every day for. . .? . . two weeks? or more? I've lost track. We've had a couple of breaks in the rain, but then it picks up where it left off, and the skies weep all over us again. We had a break in the rain this afternoon, and I took the dogs out back and let them run around the yard. They chased and ran, and chased and ran, and then chased and ran some more! While they ran, I walked circles around our big, back yard. The exercise was wonderful for all three of us. We got in just as it started to rain again. Later, when it let up for a while, we went back out and did it all over again.

My neighbor, Jo, came over this morning and— compliments of my dear friend Janelle, who supplied the teapot and tea cups for my Christmas present—Jo and I sipped Empress blend tea from Victoria, British Columbia, (the same tea they serve at the Empress Hotel) out of paper-thin Haviland China teacups from Limoges, France, poured from a Crown Dorset China teapot made in Staffordshire England. Eat your heart out, Queen Elizabeth! I told Jo to pretend we were at the Empress Hotel in Victoria, having high tea. I served store-bought, shortbread cookies, and Jo said she was really disappointed that I hadn't made the fancy cakes and pastries that go with high tea. Picky, picky, picky! Oh, well, you can't win 'em all. I made the mistake of leaving the cookies on the coffee table while Jo and I went out to look at Harry's new toy, and Schatze and Trudy helped themselves to the cookies. I guess they were upset at being left out of the party. So much for 'high tea' in this household. It completely went to the dogs!

December 10, 2001

We finally got a break from the rain—it snowed! When I got up at 3:30 a.m. to let the dogs out, it was just starting to drift lazily down. When I got up again at 7:00 a.m., a three-quarter-inch blanket of white covered everything, and it looked like a Christmas card. I should have taken pictures, but by the time I took care of the goat and cats, walked the dogs again, took my shower and got dressed, it had started to melt. By noon, it was all gone, and the temperature was up to a toasty 39 degrees. Oh, well, next time.

About six weeks ago when winter weather started getting serious, the tire shops were swamped with people getting studded tires. I waited until today to get mine and was in and out, in about 30 minutes. The young man who drove my truck into the tire bay area was attacked from the back by both dogs and almost licked to death. I was watching from the waiting room, and he was leaning forward over the steering wheel as far as possible, laughing like crazy, while trying to avoid the fastest, quick-draw tongues in the West, and drive the truck. No small feat! I should have warned him, but that would have spoiled all the fun. That young feller fer sure got his ears washed! Some guard dogs! They don't care who steals my truck!

Trudy is a sweet little dog, and really smart, but at a year old, she has a lot of puppy left in her. I know I'm spoiled because Schatze has never torn up anything in the house or in my truck. Schatze *will* snitch food if I leave it down low and available, but otherwise, she has never gotten into anything or damaged anything. Not so with Trudy! She can think of more things to get into. Yesterday, she grabbed one of the long leaves on my Orchid plant and tipped the whole thing over on the carpet, scattering dirt, bark and gravel. Today, she got into the kindling box and chewed up kindling across the carpet. Last week I left her in the back of the pickup with the camper shell closed, figuring she couldn't get into too much. Wrong. She found a piece of foam rubber and made confetti out of it. When I tell her something is a "no, no," she usually doesn't do it again—she finds something new and different. She's very imaginative and inventive. It takes two to three years to get a dog well-trained, so I've got my work cut out for me.

I have to say, she's worth the effort. Just watching the antics of Schatze and Trudy as they play, brings a lot of laughter into my life, and laughter is good medicine. Both dogs like to cuddle with me in my chair in the evenings, and that is really a chair full. But tonight, they can't get up here because I'm on the computer, so they gave me a disgusted look and went to their beds.

Last week, I went to a Christmas luncheon at Wolf Creek, with one of our church groups. The fellowship was fun, but the food was the worst I have ever eaten. The meatloaf was dried out and sliced paper-thin, with a crust that could only be described as "lightly burned." The mashed potatoes were so thin and watery they could have been better eaten with a spoon than with a fork. I only took a couple of bites of the potatoes and ate a small part of the meatloaf, then brought most of it home for the dogs. They sniffed it suspiciously, then looked back at me. They wouldn't touch it! "Don't blame me," I told them. "I didn't cook it!" In self-defense, I made meatloaf for us last weekend. I'm considering sending the left-overs to the restaurant. Maybe C.O.D.!

I'm being inundated with seed catalogs, and loving every minute of it. I don't need very many seeds, but I love looking at the catalog, reading the descriptions, and finding 'new' heirlooms. In some catalogs, it is hard to find heirloom seeds; everything is hybrid. Fortunately, more and more people are requesting unmodified heirloom seeds, so, many of the catalogs now offer them. The ones that don't have them get tossed in the trash. I'm going for all organic, heirloom seeds in my garden. It's hard to find heirloom corn, though. Almost all of it is hybrid.

I love the winter months with rain on the roof, a cozy fire in the wood stove, a cup of hot cider and a stack of seed catalogs. Ahhhh, almost heaven. Fantasy time. So why doesn't my garden look like the pictures? When one Jew meets another Jew, they say, "Next year in Jerusalem. . .," and it is a hope and a promise. When I look at seed catalogs, I say, "Next spring in my garden. . ." Actually, that's more of a hope than a promise!

I'm sending you a Christmas quiz I found. Name the twenty, well-known, Christmas songs being described. When I did the quiz at our Christmas party, I got all twenty. (I do well with songs, but don't ask me about anything else.) See how you do, and I'll send you the answers in the next letter. . . if I remember. *

1) Quadruped with crimson proboscis.

2) 8:00 p.m. to 6:00 a.m. without noise.

3) Minuscule Hamlet in the Near East.

4) Ancient benevolent sovereign.

5) Adorn the vestibule.

6) Exuberance directed to the Planet.

7) Listen, aerial Spirits announcing.

8) Trio of Monarchs.

9) Yonder in the hay rack.

10) Cherubim audited from aloft.

11) Assemble, everyone who believes.

12) Hallowed post-Meridian.

13) Fantasies of a colorless December 25.

14) Tintinnabulations.

15) A dozen, 24-hour, Yule periods.

16) Befell during the transparent bewitching hour.

17) Homo Sapiens of crystallized vapor.

18) Desire a pair of incisors on December 25.

19) I spied a maternal parent osculating

20) Perambulating through a December Solstice fantasy.

I've collected quotes and saying for years, and don't know who said most of them, but I'll pass on a few of my favorites.

Money will buy a fine dog, but only love will make its tail wag.

Only when we walk in the dark do we see the stars.

Life was simpler back when anyone who could tie a square knot could repair a clothes dryer.

Laughter is a tranquilizer with no side affects.

December 31, 2001

I didn't get very far with my end-of-the-year letter, but I couldn't let the year go out without writing *something*! As I've said before, whatever you are doing on the last day of the year will be what you will be doing the following year. I certainly hope not! I ended the year by washing three loads of laundry, changing sheets on the bed, cleaning the wood stove (a daily task). I took apart and re-did the Christmas flower arrangement, cleaned the kitchen, made a BIG pot of turkey soup from the Christmas turkey, gave myself a permanent and haircut, bathed Schatze, unpacked two boxes of records, put away the last of the Christmas decorations, took care of my animals and my neighbors animals, picked up the coffee grounds from Atlas Espresso (for my garden) and went grocery shopping. Whew! I couldn't handle many days like that!

The last day of 2001, and a whole new year ahead without any foul-ups—yet! Maybe that is why everyone is so happy and hopeful about a new year. A clean slate. A new start. Hope. Hope that family ties will be strengthened, illnesses healed, health renewed, finances improved, friendships increased. And for some, a more prayerful, closer walk with Christ.

May you have a safe and Happy 2002, and may God bless and keep you throughout the New year.

Shirlene and Harry

*Answers for Christmas songs. 1) Rudolph 2) Silent Night 3) O' Little Town of Bethlehem 4) God King Winsaslaus 5) Deck The Halls 6) Joy To The World 7) Hark, The Herald Angels Sing 8) We Three King 9) Away in a Manger 10) What Child is This? 11) O' Come all Ye Faithful 12) Oh, Holy Night 13) White Christmas 14) Jingle Bells 15) Twelve Days of Christmas 16) It Came Upon A Midnight Clear 17) Frosty The Snow Man 18) All I Want For Christmas Is My Two Front Teeth 19) I Saw Mommy Kissing Santa Claus 20) Walking In a Winter Wonderland.

Part Three

2002

...and Family

Lester O. "Ozzie" McKinney (Dad), E. Shirlene McKinney,
and Kelly M. McKinney

Dad – Lester O. "Ozzie" McKinney
Doing what he loved best

The Radulski Family, 2003
Derek and Kelly with Brantley and Parker

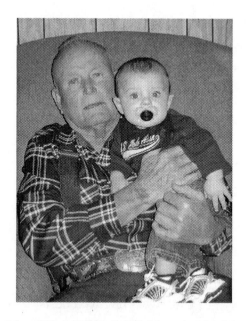

Lloyd E. Meddock (Shirlene's Uncle),
and Great-Grandon Jacob Kluenker (Erica's baby)

Diane Meddock-Allmer (Shirlene's cousin)
and her husband, Ted Allmer
with their daughters Erica Kluenker and Melissa Baker

Harry Ferguson (center, back) with his sister, Beulah,
her husband, Raymond, and their grandchildren,
Victoria and Nathan
July 8, 2004

George and Penny Pemberton, December 2004
George is Mozelle's son and is second cousin to Shirlene

Monzelle Lynch, 1956
George Pemberton's mother and
Great Aunt to Shirlene McKinney

January 1, 2002

Dear Friends and Family,

HAPPY NEW YEAR!!!! To-
day, I started the New Year watching the Rose Bowl
Parade, then spent the next five hours in the kitchen preparing a
big dinner. We had baked ham, scalloped potatoes, baked
beans, sweet potatoes, hot biscuits and fruit salad. How come
you weren't here for dinner? It's nice to fix the big dinners for
the holidays, but I sure wouldn't want to eat that way all year
long. I also wouldn't want to spend five hours a day on my feet
in the kitchen.

Our little town of Merlin is right up there with the big
city elites! We now have a coffee kiosk, the aforementioned
Atlas Espresso. The day they opened, I stopped by and asked
what they were going to do with their used coffee grounds, and
arranged to pick them up. I go just about every other day and
get 20-30 pounds of used coffee grounds that I am putting on
my garden. Next, I'll put them on the roses, around the fruit
trees, and anywhere else I can think of. The earthworms love
them. Any fishermen out there? Dump your used coffee
grounds in a specific area, and you'll have all the fishing
worms you will ever need.

It's almost 4:00 p.m. and time to go feed my neighbor's
dogs, so don't go 'way. I'll be back, soon.

(I'm back, already and you didn't even miss me!) When
I boiled the turkey carcass, I had left over bits of turkey that
didn't go into the soup, so that is Holiday treats for the animals.
I took some over to Sabrina and King (my neighbor's dogs) and
mixed it with their dog food. Schatze and Trudy had a bowl of
turkey earlier today, they have some left for tomorrow, and I

fed all of my (4) cats turkey instead of cat food. They didn't
seem to mind one bit.

Harry has been after me to put Clementine in the upper
pasture where we are building the garden enclosure and chicken
coop. I couldn't do it previously because our little fruit trees
still had leaves on them, and I knew she would destroy the trees
by eating the leaves, but now, the leaves are all gone. I told
Harry, "If you'll move my potted plants out of the pasture so
Clementine can't eat them, I'll put her in the pasture this
afternoon, providing you'll help watch for rain. If it starts to
rain, either get Clementine back in her pen, or let me know it is
raining, and I'll put her back. Goats don't like to be wet, and
she shouldn't be out in the rain."

"Okay," he agreed. He was in the pasture, working inside the chicken coop, with the doors and windows cut out, so I
knew he could instantly see if it started raining.

When I looked out an hour later, it was pouring rain,
and Clementine was running back and forth along the fence.
Harry was oblivious. I grabbed my coat and old yard shoes and
ran for the pasture. When I got to the back gate, Clementine
was soaking wet and came running to meet me. Poor baby. She
knew I was coming to help her. I walked her back to her pen,
and she immediately ran into the shed to get out of the rain. I
won't be putting her in the pasture again unless I know it isn't
going to rain. No more trusting her care to Harry!

"After eleven days of holiday vacation, Harry returns to
work tomorrow and is bemoaning the fact. Someone wanted to
know when I get my vacation? Obvious answer—when Harry
goes back to work! Any woman reading this will know exactly
what I'm talking about.

For any of you who have a fireplace or wood stove with
glass doors, I've found an easy way to clean the glass. I used to

wait until the glass was cold, then it was a job of scrubbing and scraping the burned-on soot and smoke. I found if I cleaned while the glass is still warm (not *hot!*) the residue wipes off quite easily. Since I clean the glass door every day so we can see the fire, it made a big difference in the amount of scrubbing I have to do.

Oregon has a sports team called the Ducks—I presume because of all the rain we get in Oregon. This summer, when I was in the Rogue River Park, I watched *real* ducks waddle from the park down to the water, their behinds swaying from one side to the other. I thought naming a sports team "Ducks" was rather strange, until I was recently waiting at a stop light in Grants Pass. A short, portly fellow passed in front of my vehicle. His green wind-breaker jacket hanging down over his very ample, swaying posterior, was emblazoned with the word "Ducks." I immediately saw the connection. So maybe it's more than just the rain?

During this year, I hope to find a good, hand clinic and heart specialist (on the West Coast) to get both things, heart and hand, "fixed." If you have a prayer list, keep those items on it, please.

January 2, 2002

It rained yesterday, last night and into the early hours of this morning, but the sun is out now in all its glory. What a way to kick off the New Year! Hope your own New Year is off to a great start, and will continue that way. Our love and prayers,

Shirlene, Harry, et al

January 21, 2002

Dear Friends and Family,

    The goat is locked safely in her shed, the cats are in the garage, and the dogs went willingly to their snugly beds. A cozy fire is burning, and all is quiet here. A good time to write letters. It's a good thing I don't watch TV, or I'd never get any letters written.

    It is trying to snow tonight, but not having much success. Late this afternoon, while visiting friends who live on top of one of the surrounding mountains, it started snowing up there, but when I got back down on the valley floor, we had big, slushy flakes that melted as soon as they hit the ground. Maybe, if it gets a little bit colder tonight, we might have a ground covering in the morning. When we had heavy rains earlier this month, our pretty, little creek disappeared and became a roaring river. However, it lasted less than a week and is now running normally again. . . a little deeper than summer run, but still wade-able.

    The friends I visited this afternoon told me their neighbor had a cougar in his yard recently, and when he was building his house, a bear visited their garbage cans. Did I mention that we live *in* the mountains? All of the usual animals are around this area; the cute and cuddly, and the not-so-cute and cuddly. Predators such as cougars and bears usually stay at the higher elevations, unless they happen to get really hungry, and we happen to leave a tasty morsel out for them such as a nice, fat, little goat, or a cat or small dog. That's why my animals are safely locked away every night, so they won't become the main course on some predator's menu.

    January brought reminders from the vet's office that my animals all need shots. With as many animals as I now have, that presents a sizable cost, so I went to our local Grange, bought the shots and have been giving booster shots to Schatze, Mischief, C.C., and Suzy. Trudy gets her booster shot in February, as does Clementine. I'll have to take them to the vet for rabies, but for the rest of the shots, I'm getting to be a real whiz with the needle. Not one of them flinched or gave any indication they knew they had a shot! Not bad for an amateur. Sissy, sad to say, has disappeared. I'm hoping someone stole her and gave her a good home, because the other option is that a predator got her.

The chicken coop is s-l-o-w-l-y but surely getting finished and moved into position on the north side of the garden. I can hardly wait to get my chickens, but it will probably be another month before it is ready. We needed doors for the chicken coop and will need a couple for our goat shed, so I contacted a local door company and got three, nice, three-foot metal, outside doors, for $20.00 (not each - all three for $20.00!) They were damaged and have a couple of dents in them, but not very noticeable, and I doubt the chickens or goat will complain. I was thrilled with the price.

When Trudy came here two months ago, she had multiple problems, but she is making so much progress. She shook all the time and cowered every time anyone came near her. She no longer does that, and she often runs up to me to be petted. She is gradually getting over the panic attacks when I get out of her sight, but that is something that we still have to work on. At first, I couldn't leave her at all. Now I can leave her for a few minutes at a time without her going ballistic and tearing up something. It takes time and patience. I figure it will probably take a year, but she is smart and anxious to learn. She and Schatze have become such good buddies, so I guess it is worth the effort.

Someone called earlier today and I tried to use the Huckleberry Finn psychology to convince them I was having a great time cleaning the refrigerator, an-n-n-d for a fee, I *might* consider letting them help me. They didn't buy it! Literally! So, I got to have al-l-l that fun, all by myself. I don't know how that refrigerator gets so messy, so fast. I think someone sneaks in at night while I am sleeping, and messes it up. Harry comes home at 2:00 a.m., so he is the most likely suspect. Or, maybe, Clementine comes in for a midnight snack.

Have you ever seen a ginger root? Some of them have a main part and then nubby, knobs off the end or sides. The one I bought recently had the knobs on the end. When Harry wanted to know what it was, I told him, "It's the foot and toes off of a club-footed Leprechaun!" He said, "Right!" and left the room shaking his head like he didn't believe me. I don't know why he doesn't take my answers more seriously.

January 26, 2002

The snow we didn't get last week is trying to come down now, but it is slushy, as usual, so it won't last. Since we don't have snow very often, it's nice to watch big, fluffy flakes, even if they do melt almost immediately. I'm glad it's not a regular, permanent part of our winter.

When I call the cats to lock them up for the night, they are often reluctant to come into the garage, but tonight, with snowflakes covering their backsides, they were more than ready.

With the chicken coop nearing completion, hopefully before the end of February, I ordered my baby chickens today. I feel like a kid awaiting Christmas! I ordered twelve Buff Brahmas, ten Aracuanas and twelve Buff Brahma Bantams, and will get them in March. I won't be able to get my ten guineas until late May or June, as Guineas don't lay or hatch until after all danger of frost is past. Smart birds! I was going to order through a catalog hatchery, but they were too expensive, and they require a *minimum* of 30 guineas, a *minimum* of 25 bantams, etc. I don't have room for that many. I ordered locally and can get smaller batches at lower prices. I've been saving my "chicken" money, a few dollars here and there, all winter. By the time the chicks are ready to pick up, I will have the money to pay for them.

There were so many beautiful chickens I could have ordered 100 or more, just getting ten of each different variety, IF I had the space. Columbian Wyandotts are beautiful, but I settled on the Buff Brahmas because they aren't affected by cold weather and (supposedly) will lay right through the winter months. The Aracuanas are the chickens from *way* south of the border—Chili, South America—that lay multi-colored "Easter" eggs. (I think they cluck and crow in Spanish. . . or would that be Portuguese?) And the Buff Brahma Bantams? Well, let's just say I like bantams! If I could only have a few chickens of one breed, I would choose bantams. Their eggs are much smaller, but I think they have better flavor. Besides, the bantams are cute!

A filling came out of one of my teeth, so I went to the dentist, yesterday, to have it fixed. I figured they would want to do a lot of excess, *expensive* work on my teeth, and I was right. When I walked into their plush office with four dentists available, I knew right away I was in trouble. Sure enough, they didn't just want to drill and replace my filling. They wanted to also remove and replace all of my bridgework, to the tune of $2,000.00 dollars! I could tell the dentist wasn't very happy with me when I said "no," and only authorized the filling to be replaced for $214.00. (I found out later, that was about double what another dentist would have charged.) Let someone else pay for their fancy offices! It isn't the dental work I mind, it is the high-pressure sales tactics they use. It's all about making money.

The dentist shot me full of anesthesia to deaden my mouth, and I think he got carried away because my whole face was numb for over twelve hours. Maybe he was getting even because I refused the excessive work. He drilled, filled, and said, "Bite down. Now, how does that feel?" Right! As if I could feel anything. I told him, "umg glb tmk," and he either understood perfectly or didn't give a Tinker's damn, and I think it was the latter.

I'm still picking up coffee grounds at the coffee kiosk and dumping them in all the flower beds and garden areas. I wish I had a whole lot more to spread around the plants. When I put the coffee grounds on my salad-and-herb garden out back of the house, I noticed that the garlic is poking through the ground, escaping from its winter imprisonment, and I still have lettuce, pac Choi, parsley and a few onions and carrots that didn't freeze, in spite of the snow! I should have planted Kale, but I'll do that this coming fall. Our love and prayers,

Shirlene & Harry

February 6, 2002

Dear Friends and Family,

Recently, Harry was reading the classified section of the newspaper and when he came to the lost and found section he said, "Someone has an ad in here for a lost sheep."

"Probably Little Bo Peep," I quipped. It was a couple of seconds before that registered.

In the same classified section, there was an ad for free roosters. I called and asked if they also had some hens. "Yes, but they aren't free." I bought three Light Brahmas. They are white with a black and white "collar" and black tail feathers. They didn't have any roosters of the same breed, and they wouldn't sell me the hens unless I took one of the roosters off their hands, so I chose a little Mille Fleur as my free rooster. He's about half the size of the hens, so I doubt he will be able to 'service' them. However, he is a pretty little bird with reddish feathers tipped in white, full, black, tail feathers and heavily feathered feet. Because of the feathers on his feet, he picks his feet up high when walking, giving him the appearance of dancing. Since "Mille Fleur" sounded French, (its a Belgian breed), annnnd he's a "dancer," I named him Maurice Chevalier!

I went early in the day to pick out the chickens I wanted, and their owner asked if I could leave the cage and come back for them later, as they would be easier to catch late in the afternoon. I said, "Sure, what time?" and he told me to come back after 3:30 p.m. By the time I got back, it was almost 4:00 p.m. and he had the chickens in the cage. I noticed he had changed clothes. He said, "When I went to catch that little Mille Fleur, he headed for the creek. I followed him, and when I hit that slippery bank, my feet went out from under me, and I slid right down into the creek." *He* probably didn't think it was all that funny. You would have been proud of me. I didn't laugh until I was in my truck and going out their gate (ah, such control!), and then the picture of his sliding down the creek bank on his rear end, right into the creek, kept me laughing all the way home.

We've been dumping our kitchen garbage in the garden area and covering it with coffee grounds that I pick up from the kiosk. When I let the chickens out in the morning, it doesn't take them very long to find their way into the garden area. They scratch, cluck, scratch, peck their way all around that garden enclosure, and every so often Maurice stops, stretches his little neck as high as possible (I think he stands on his tip-toes!) and crows! He's the Mickey Rooney of the chicken kingdom.

Usually, when moving chickens, they won't lay for a couple of weeks, but these little hens started laying the day after we moved them, and we're collecting two or three eggs a day. And boy, do these free-range, organic eggs taste good!

My neighbor, Jo, called this morning and said she was coming over. I had some information I wanted to give her, so I said, "When you get here, remind me, or I may forget to give it to you". She said, "Well, who's going to remind me to remind you?" I laughed, and she continued, "Honestly, sometimes I feel like a half-wit!"

"Me, too. But, that's okay. If you're a half-wit and I'm a half-wit, together we make a whole-wit!"

Our weather here goes from colder than a witch's petu-tie to warm and wet. Typical winter. We don't usually get much wind here, but this afternoon, we had about half-an-hour of strong wind that blew my newspaper "mulch" all over this one-and-one-third acre (boy do I have a mess to pick up), knocked out the power a couple of times and the sky got a threatening lead-gray. I was praying it wouldn't rain until after I got the animals fed and locked up for the night. When I went out, a few drops started to splat-splatter, but I hurried and got all my "babies" fed and locked up for the night, and got the dogs out for a 'potty break,' before the rain hit. Now, the dogs and I are enjoying our crackling fire and listening to the rain splashing against the windows.

February 25, 2002

The month of February always gets away from me. I think it's because it is such a short month. All of a sudden, I wake up and realize it is March and time to start my indoor seeds. I've been going through last year's seeds, taking inventory and trying to figure out what I'll plant this year. For the things I want to plant, I think I need an extra five acres and about six more sets of hands to take care of it! Obviously, something has to go! (I wish it were the gophers! They could 'go' anytime!)

Crocus bulbs should start blooming by next week, followed closely by the daffodils and tulips. I hope to get my sweet peas in the ground within the next couple of weeks, and will plant my Oregon Sugar Snap and Sugar Ann Peas, as soon as I get the chickens out of the garden area. Harry is working on the chicken run, which is at the east side of the garden (drawing enclosed), and should have it done in a couple of weeks, just in time for me to start planting.

One of the visiting cats disappeared and I have been really concerned about her. Then, one night she came in across the meadow, meowing all the way. I fed her and locked her in the garage for 24 hours, while I managed to put a collar on her, with my phone number, and give her a booster shot. By the next morning, she was howling frantically to get out. From the desperation in her cries, I suspected she may have had kittens hidden and needed to get to them, so, I let her out, and she ran lickety-split to the blackberry brambles by the creek, where she disappeared. I didn't see her for about three weeks. After locking her up and giving her a shot, she doesn't trust me very much. Can't say I blame her.

I started putting cat food on the back deck at night, after all my cats were locked up, and the food has been gone every morning. I wasn't sure if I was feeding Sissy, a racoon, or a possum, so I placed a newspaper on the deck, sifted flour all over it and set the cat food in the middle of the paper. The next morning, I had nice, white, kitty-cat paw prints all over the deck, so now I've narrowed the choices down. I'm either feeding my estranged cat or one of my neighbor's cats! (Today the missing cat came to the front porch and Mischief and my dogs chased her off. At least I know she is alive.)

In the three months I've had her, Trudy has settled in pretty well. She doesn't shake and tremble all the time the way she did when I first got her. I can go outside to lock up the animals and leave her loose in the house, without her tearing up anything, and when I go shopping, I have been able to leave her in the pickup for longer periods of time, with nothing destroyed. She still doesn't like for me to be out of her sight, but she doesn't have panic attacks like she did at first, so that's progress!

After almost five months of hassles, our refinance finally closed. It only saved us about $60 per month on our payment, but it will save us a good chunk of interest over a period of years, so I guess it was worth the stress. I know all lending institutions send their underwriters to a special school, before they become qualified. The main course is, "How To Keep Your Client Stressed Out, In Four Easy Lessons." The first lesson consists of keeping your client's folder shuffled to the bottom of the stack. The second lesson is, ordering as many pay-offs as possible, and having your client pay for them. Third, ordering the wrong type of appraisal, resulting in re-ordering and a longer waiting period, and fourth, requesting that the client furnish redundant paperwork. All underwriters are well-trained in these areas.

I'm kidding. Actually, we had a really nice underwriter who did everything possible to get the loan through. The delays, I'm sure, were not her fault.

I had problems with chest pains last night and couldn't sleep, so I finally got up at 2:00 a.m. and took an aspirin, which resulted in my being sick the remainder of the night and hanging over the commode, with nothing coming up. I still don't feel like dancing the tango, but I'm sure tomorrow will be better!! I guess I'm going to have to do something about this heart arrhythmia. It's becoming a real pain in the. . . chest. Ha! You thought I was going to say another area, didn't you? Anyway, if you have a prayer list, keep me in prayer and, maybe, I can find a "fix-it mechanic!"

Meanwhile, know that I am praying for *you*. I have a prayer list, and I take it with me when I take the dogs out for their afternoon exercise. While they run around this half-plus acre of yard, I walk around it, praying for each person on the list. I call it my prayer walk, and the good Lord and I have some interesting talks during those afternoon prayer walks. You are daily on my mind, in my heart and definitely in my prayers. May His hand be upon you in all that you do, and may He keep you safe and well.

Sending our love from the "Funny Farm,"

Shirlene, Harry & the Zoo !

March 3, 2002

Dear Friends & Family,

My daffodils popped open on the first of March, like musicians responding to a conductor's baton! They will continue to bloom most of this month, then my tulips will follow the parade. I've been buying fresh flowers for the house, all winter, so it is nice to have fresh-cut flowers from the yard.

March came in like the proverbial lamb, so if that cliche' holds true, we're in for a blizzard around the end of this month. Verrrrrry doubtful. Right now, we're having such beautiful spring weather, temperatures in the fifty-sixty-and seventy degrees during the day, but dropping down to the twenties at night. Today was a seventy-degree day, and I couldn't contain myself. I was outside planting flowers!

I bought fifty-two steel T-post, yesterday, and Harry put them, 4-to-a-tree, around each of our thirteen little fruit trees. Today, I planted mustard around the trees to put some nitrogen in the soil, and hope to get netting around them soon, in an effort to keep the deer from eating them like they did last year. No sooner did the trees get a few leaves than the deer came through and stripped them. If any of you are deer hunters, you're welcome to come and visit us. You can fill your deer tag, right here in our yard! You can go 'Coon hunting here, too, and how about gopher hunting? Bet you've never had tasty, gopher stew! Yum! (I'll furnish a recipe, *free!*) And, for those of you who have never hunted before, we'll take you Snipe hunting. Such fun!

Last week I was working in the yard and had both dogs outside with me, so they could get some fresh air and sunshine. Trudy wanders the property, checks out the chickens, chases the cats, teases the goat, and tries to get Schatze to chase her, but she still likes to know where I am, so every now and then, she comes to check on me. Not Schatze! She watches until she's sure I'm busy and not watching *her*, and then she sneaks off. I suddenly realized I hadn't seen her for quite some time. I toured the entire property, calling "here Schatze," to no avail. Thinking, perhaps, she had sneaked into the house when I came in to get a drink, I searched the entire house. No Schatze. Finally, I got in the car and started driving the roads.

Our property is fenced on three sides, but not out back where the creek runs through. Schatze had crossed the creek, climbed the steep, rocky bank on the other side, gone through our neighbors unfenced yard and kept going. I finally found her, about a half mile down Ward Road, tootling down the road, enjoying the scenery and singing "On The Road Again." Typical Wire Terrier. They love to wander.

Both dogs were out on the property with us today while Harry worked on the chicken yard, and I planted and raked. I made sure I kept a close eye on Schatze. The dogs ran and chased and chased and ran around this whole property. When we finally came in, they were two pooped pups. They plopped down on the carpet and snoozed out. This is such an ideal place for them to run and play.

Mischief is my hunter, and she caught something the other day, but I couldn't tell if it was a mouse or a small gopher. When I tried to get close enough to see what she had, she ran away. Several times, I've made her turn loose birds she caught, so now, instead of coming to show me her prize, she runs and hides while she eats it. What she doesn't understand is, if it was a gopher, I was going to give her a raise in pay!

A friend of mine, from church, had her three-year-old grandson visiting for the weekend. He spotted a picture on her dresser and asked, "Grandma, who's that?"

"That was me, when I graduated from high school."

He turned back to the picture and studied it for some time. Looking back at his grandmother, he asked, "What happened?"

The same grandson, at his third birthday, got a new shirt. His grandpa was wearing a new western shirt and teased the grandson, "Do you want to trade shirts?"

The grandson looked up at his grandpa. "No, grandpa. Your shirt's ugly."

I left my sourdough starter on the counter this morning before we left for church. By the time we came home, it was bubbling and ready to work, so I made fresh bread this afternoon. Not a package mix, and not done in a bread machine! The "old fashioned" way. Back in the late 1970's, I baked all my own bread, but got out of the habit in the last twenty years. Now, I'm having to practice a bit to get the "touch" back again. The hardest part is remembering to take out part of the starter for the next batch!

We've had a few birds checking out the bird houses. One little sparrow went inside while her mate sat on the roof and kept watch. Soon she hopped back out and chattered to him. *"It's not nearly as big as the real estate lady made it sound! No family room, and only one bath!"* But I guess they decided to "buy" it anyway, because she went back in. When she didn't come out for some time, he hopped down on the perch and stuck his head inside. *"What* are *you doing in there?"*

"Cleaning house, of course. The previous tenants left this place in a mess!"

March 5, 2002

Harry brought in wood for the stove. The wood had holes in it, and the holes had bugs in them, so I quickly threw it in the stove. When you come to see us, I'll fix you my gourmet special— roast termites! Yum! Well, it can't be much worse than chocolate-covered ants, grasshoppers, or snails, and people eat *those*.

Our sunshine turned gray, and the skies are weeping again. Can't complain though. We need the rain, and we had a whole week of warm, sunny weather. Anyway, this is my week to run errands, and I'd rather do that in rainy weather when I can't be outside, and save my stay-at-home time for nice days when I can work in the garden and yard. Besides, I always have plenty of things to do in the house.

I've been doing those "thankless" jobs that you can't see. . . like cleaning out cupboards. It needs to be done, but, when you're through, nobody can see what you've done, so you're the only one who knows. Seems to me there ought to be some kind of roadside billboard that could be posted with daily up-dates— *Cleaned cupboards today! Ta Da!*—and then, everyone would know, and you would have some sense of satisfaction. Doesn't do any good to tell your husband, "Honey, I cleaned cupboards today." You won't know if his "grunt" is an acknowledgment of what you said, or just gas. Probably the latter.

The dogs have a whole box of toys, but, like kids, they prefer to fight over one. *"Mom, Schatze won't share!"*

"Well, come here, Trudy, and I'll throw this toy for you." Then Schatze drops the toy she is playing with and goes to take away the one Trudy has. I try to tell her she has to share, but she just glares at me. *"Mine!"* Sigh! The terrible "twos."

March 15, 2002

What I like about this area is that we have four seasons...and we had at least three of them today! When I got up this morning, it was thirty-three degrees and snowing lightly. It didn't stick, just drifted down and melted. A couple of hours later the temperature rose and we had brilliant sunshine. A little later, we still had the sunshine, but it was also raining. From long johns to shorts to rain gear, in one day! Don't like the weather? Wait around a little while. It will change. At least it isn't boring.

I wanted to get my peas and celery planted, but it has been too rainy to work the soil, so I've left the garden gate open for the chickens. They alternate between their new yard and my garden area. I had planned on starting some of my indoor garden and flower seeds this week, but I may go out of town the end of this month (a sort of belated, birthday trip), so I can't start my seeds until I get back, or they will all die while I'm away. Once the gardening starts, I have to be here.

I went to a holistic doctor in Medford this week, and while I was there, the nurse practitioner did a bone density test. When she got the results, she said, "Wow! That's on the chart exactly where *my* test results were." No osteoporosis! I felt pretty good about that since I am at least twenty years older than the nurse. Several years ago a medical doctor told me I had osteoporosis, based on my age alone, even though he never checked me for it. Using *his* method of determination, I classified him a Neanderthal!

Most of my medical appointments in the past five years have been fifteen minute sessions, spent with a doctor staring at fly specs on the wall somewhere above and in back of my head, not hearing a word I said, then handing me three prescriptions immediately after I have told him I don't do drugs, and shuffling me back out the door with no more answers than when I entered.

The holistic/medical doctor I went to last week spent two hours with me, did a very thorough examination, ran some tests and actually *listened* to what I was saying and communicated with me! Amazing! It seems to me I remember this kind of medical practice when I was growing up, but sadly, we have now evolved (digressed would be a better word) to fifteen-minute-revolving-door medicine.

I told the doctor what I have been doing, the vitamins and supplements I have been taking, etc; and she said, "You're on the right track. We'll do some more tests to see exactly what you are lacking and what you need, but, for right now, just keep on doing what you've been doing." I guess all the research and reading I've been doing hasn't been a total waste. Unfortunately, I've been using the "shotgun method." Now, maybe I can get more specific answers.

March 18, 2002

Since today was my birthday, I wanted to do something pleasurable, so, in addition to errands I had to run, I went to Farmer's Supply to see what kind of baby chicks they had. "Orpingtons," *no, thanks;* "Sex Links," *no, thanks*; "Cornish Rocks," *no, thanks*; "Barred Rocks," *no, thanks;* "Aracuanas," . . . "Aracuanas?" That got my attention.

"How many did you want?"

"Oh, only about six, I guess." He had seven of them left, and I couldn't possibly leave that one little chick all alone, so I bought myself seven baby chicks for my birthday! Aracuanas are really pretty, very individual and no two are alike. They are unbelievably cute. Light-tan, reddish-brown, and one black chick, decorated with varying stripes and feather patterns, running around on toothpick legs, trying to learn to scratch. It's about like watching a baby learn to walk. They scratch, scratch, get out of balance and fall over, get up and try again.

Our financial news item is that we received a check from Solomon Smith Barney, and we are trying to decide if we should use it towards a trip to the Bahamas, Harry's early retirement, or other frivolous endeavors. The check says "Two signatures required if over $25,000.00," and both signatures are on the check. I was going to get the cash, but I wasn't sure our bank could handle a check of this magnitude. I've never before received one quite like it. The check is for four cents! In the end, I've decided to frame it!

March 19, 2002

An early doctor appointment in Medford, this morning, got me up before the chickens. Literally! Maurice's cock-a-doodle-doo was a bit on the sleepy side when I let them out. It sounded more like "err-a-err-a-auuuug," I completely agree!

The doctor ran some tests, but I won't get the lab results back for two weeks. She said, "I want you to go on a special diet for the next three weeks." Then, she gave me a list of foods I couldn't eat . . . no wheat (no morning toast?), eggs, dairy products, red meat (don't eat that anyway), no sweets (sigh!), no shellfish, no alcohol (no problem), no caffeine, no peanuts (there goes the peanut butter), and no potatoes! Now, that last one really hurt. When you hit an Irishman in the potato basket, that's a low blow. It would have been a shorter list if she's said what I *can* eat. *No-o-o--t much!* The treatment may be worse than the illness.

I suppose I'd better close this gab session and get ready for a busy day tomorrow, while the nice weather lasts. Hope everyone and everything is well in your neck of the woods. Until next time, keep your powder dry, and keep the outhouse door locked!

Our love and prayers,

Shirlene and Harry

March 23, 2002

D ear Friends and Family,

Garden season has started, so I went to the Grange and bought a variety of natural fertilizers: Bone meal, alfalfa meal, blood meal, phosphorus, greensand, granite, cottonseed meal, fish emulsion and one or two others I can't remember. It occurred to me that I have spent more on fertilizers this past year than I have spent on cologne. Now that's what I'd call a stinky situation!

I don't know if you are familiar with the rose people, *Jackson & Perkins*, or not, but they have been supplying top quality roses for many years—and they are located in Medford. Last time I was in Medford to do some shopping, I stopped by the *Jackson & Perkins* outlet store. Many of the hybrid roses, while very pretty, have no fragrance. They've had all the 'scent' bred out of them. English roses are the old, heirloom varieties that have the strong, rose fragrance, and they are the ones that are used to make potpourri. I bought three English roses, and I can hardly wait to get them planted and have them blooming. Maybe I can spread English rose petals on the garden and "overpower" the fertilizer smell! (Actually, the only natural fertilizer that has any smell is fish emulsion, and that one stinks badly enough to make up for all the rest.)

Before the walkway between the garden, chicken yard and chicken coop, was fenced over the top, one of our resident blue jays discovered a Fast Food Fly-In. He landed on the roof of the chicken coop, dropped down to the doorway ramp, then hopped through the open doorway into the coop, where there is ample food and water. A couple of times our help-yourself freeloader made a wrong turn coming back out and wound up in the chicken yard, which *is* fenced over the top. Then, he couldn't find his way back out. Boy, was he one panicked bird when I went out there. I cornered him and managed to grab him, then carried him to the open walkway and gave him a boost skyward. He didn't even stop to say thank you.

Harry finally has the shingles on the chicken coop—no more leaking roof! He is getting ready to paint it, and the wire is now over the walkway. That's going to be one frustrated blue jay!

My baby Aracuanas are doing well, developing wing feathers, and flying like Kamikazes. They run part-way down the ramp to get up speed, then are airborne to the end of the enclosure. Their landings aren't necessarily the most graceful, but they recover, run back to the ramp and do it all over again. Practice makes perfect!

April 9, 2002

I don't recall much of what has happened between March 23, and now, except that I've been too busy to get this letter finished, so *something* must have been going on! I got peas planted, they are up and I planted broccoli and purple cabbage. My three garlic plants that I planted last fall are now two feet high, and I have tulips and daffodils in abundance.

Among other things, I acquired three, Buff Brahma hens and two, Buff Brahma roosters to add to the chicken yard. The big, Light Brahma (white) hens really gave the new little hens a bad time, and my sassy little Mille Fleur, Maurice, picked a fight with the biggest Buff Brahma rooster. He fluffed out his wings, side-stepped and "bumped" into the new (bigger) rooster. After doing it several times, the big Brahma took the challenge, and they went at it. I figured Maurice was going to get his tail feathers trounced, but when I went to check on them, the big rooster's comb was bloody from one end to the other. Maurice had a couple of battle scars, but nothing like the big guy. I had to go buy some medicine and doctor him, and keep Maurice in a cage for several days to let the newcomer heal.

Although I hated to do it, I had to find a home for Maurice and the bantam Brahma rooster. I wanted the big Brahma for producing baby chicks, so Maurice and the small Brahma went to a new home. I'm sure my neighbor appreciates that I don't have three roosters crowing 100 feet from her bedroom window. One rooster is really all my hens need.

Since Maurice has departed and the Buff Brahma is the only rooster in the hen house, he really struts his stuff. Maurice proved the new "kid" on the block is not as tough as he thinks he is, but, because he has a macho swagger and *thinks* he's tough-stuff, I've named him Rooster Cogburn!

My hands are getting progressively worse, and I finally had to admit that I am not going to be able to milk Clementine. I also had to face the fact that Clementine was lonely, and the pen and shed we had for her really were not adequate. I thought perhaps Harry would be able to build a pen for her this summer, but he has so many projects now, that it probably won't get done.

When I went to have the studded tires removed from my pickup, I became acquainted with a lady who had a neutered, male goat, (a wether) and she was looking for a companion for him. I took Clementine to her property, and she had a much better place for the goats to run and play. So, Clementine now has a playmate and (for her), a much better home. I miss her, but I know it is for the best.

Last, but not least, I have been having a lot of allergy attacks for the past five months and couldn't figure out why.

When I was cleaning my pickup and was in that small, enclosed area with all of Trudy's dog hair, I had a really bad attack. It finally dawned on me that the dog hair was the problem. I've always had Wire Haired Fox Terriers for inside dogs, and they don't shed, so I didn't know I was allergic to dog hair. I placed an ad in the paper and turned down the first six callers. Allergies or not, I wasn't about to let Trudy go someplace if I didn't feel it would be a good home for her.

Finally, a lady called that sounded like a good match, so I took Trudy to her house for a visit. She has two, teenage boys, 13 and 16, and they came home while I was there. All three were down in the floor playing with Trudy, and Trudy was ecstatic about all the attention. The 13-year-old boy said, "Mom, I think I'm in love!" The mother is a stay-at-home mom, so the dog is with her twenty-four, seven. She has previously owned a Jack Russell terrier, so it turned out to be a really good match. Schatze and I both miss Trudy, but I have cleaned my carpets and pickup of all the dog hair, and I am breathing much easier.

I really prayed for good homes for my animals before I let them go, and I feel God answered my prayers. I can go see Clementine and Trudy if I want to. However, since I think Trudy should be bonding with her new family, I probably won't do that for some time. Anyway, I'm comfortable with the fact that they are loved.

We've had such beautiful spring weather—lots of days in the seventies and eighties. Last night, it clouded over and rained, and it has rained gently, off and on today. Good! We needed it.

April 11, 2002

Solomon 2:11-12: [11] *For lo, the winter is past, the rain is over and gone;* [12] *The flowers appear on the earth; the time of the singing of birds is come, and the voice of the turtle is heard in our land.* Do turtles have voices? I must have missed the Turtle Choir when they were in town.

Our pasture is on a little hill, slightly higher than the house. At night, when I go up the hill to lock up the chickens, I take a few minutes to enjoy the view. Tonight, I stood under a canopy of silver clouds and blue sky, and slowly turned in a circle. On the east, blue and green mountains, wearing a crown of dark green trees, saw-toothed against blue-gray clouds. On the south side, pink and white blossomed trees and yellow forsythia, and a hedge of red fire bushes. On the west side were giant oaks and maples standing sentinel in the lawn, silhouetted against the creek bank and changing sky, providing a shady haven at the end of the day; and, on the north side, an old apple orchard, and our own small orchard, strutting their flowers like an Easter parade.

Truly, God put beauty all around if we take the time to stop and look.

Spring and summer are really busy here, and it seems I'm on the run from daylight to dark. With daylight savings time, my days are long. However, it is a time when the land revives and awakens after a long winter's sleep, so I guess I have to do the same. The peas that I planted are up, sweet peas have peeked through the soil, and shrubs and perennials are budding out. The grass needs mowing every five days, the pasture needs mowing, and the weeds are growing like . . . weeds! Any time you run out of something to do, come on up. I can put you to work.

I'll close by including some church jokes I found, and hope you get a chuckle or two. *Proverbs 17:22 A merry heart doeth good like a medicine, but a broken spirit drieth the bones*; so you'd better laugh, or your bones will dry up! Then you'll be singing, "Dem bones, dem bones, dem dry bones. . . ."

My love and prayers; may God keep you laughing!

Shirlene and Harry

Church jokes:

A man died and went to Heaven, dragging a large suitcase with him. Saint Peter met him at the gate. "What do you think you're doing? You can't bring anything in here."

"It's okay. I talked to the Big Boss and he said I could bring one thing with me."

Not totally convinced, Saint Peter says, "Well. . . okay. Let me see what you've got."

The man opens the suitcase and it is full of gold.

Saint Peter looks at him, incredulous. "You brought pavement?!"

Seen outside churches:

"Are you wrinkled with burdens? Come in for a faith-lift."

"Free trip to heaven! Details inside."

"God so loved the world that he did not send a committee."

"Give God what's right, not what's left."

"This church is prayer-conditioned."

"Plan ahead—it wasn't raining when Noah started building the ark."

"Having trouble sleeping? Come hear one of our sermons."

"A lot of kneeling will leave you in good standing."

April 29, 2002

Dear Friends and Family,

A couple of days of alternating soft rain and sunshine have encouraged the grass to grow tall and vividly green, but, late this afternoon, God painted the sky dark slate gray and announced a serious rain with rolls of thunder that sent Schatze hiding in her bed. After the thunder stopped, Schatze got brave enough to venture out of her bed, and she is now sleeping by my chair, snuggled up as closely as she can get to my foot.

The sky opened up and poured, and the chickens ran for the warm, dry safety of their coop. From a heavy downpour, we temporarily settled into a steady, drumming rain, then back to beating a heavy staccato on the skylights. This will be a good night for sleeping.

We got a slight break in the downpour around 7:00 p.m., and I locked up the chickens an hour early tonight. They were already in their coop, so I tossed some alfalfa and sunflower seeds on the floor for a treat, and left them happily pecking and clucking.

The Araucanas are getting bigger each day and are holding their own pretty well with the big chickens. Last week when I was cleaning the chicken coop, one of the little chicks started screeching, "Peeeep, peeeep!" which sounded very much like "Help, help!" He was doing a combination of running and flying towards the chicken coop door, with Rooster Cogburn in hot pursuit. The little one careened through the door, kicking new straw and fresh wood shavings in every direction, and dashed through the opening to the "nursery" pen just ahead of the rooster, who can't fit through the small opening. The little Araucana immediately stopped and looked back at Rooster Cogburn as if to say, *"Made it! Ha, ha! You can't get me."*

Harry still has to put a permanent fence between the nursery and main chicken pen before I can get my Guineas. We've only had a three-foot-high, temporary fence separating the 'nursery' pen and the main chicken yard. Once the Araucanas got their wings, they just yelled, "Annie, Annie over!" and flew right over the fence. The big chickens are too heavy to fly over it, or not bright enough to figure it out, but it hasn't stopped the little ones. We couldn't figure out why the temporary fence pulled loose from the building and fell down. Harry put it back up again, and before he could get out of the pen, five of the Aracuanas landed on the top of it and perched precariously while it wobbled back and forth. No wonder it fell down!

Yesterday, a hawk swooped down, looking for dinner. Good thing we fenced the top of the chicken pen, or one of my little Araucanas would have been Mr. Hawk's gourmet meal. I think he was puzzled that the chickens were there, and he couldn't get to them. He landed on our white fence and studied the situation for about ten minutes before he finally gave up and flew away. I'm sure I saw a disgusted look on his face as he flew by the dining room window.

Like the song *Tomorrow* says, May is "only a day away." From May through mid-October are the busiest months of the year for me. Summer chores have begun. I try to sleep in until 7:00 or 7:30 a.m. because I know once my feet hit the floor, I'm up and running for the rest of the day. I throw on some old clothes and go let the little chicks into their small yard, and the big chickens into the main pen. Then I feed, check all three of the chicken waterers, feed the rabbit and check her water, and head back inside for breakfast and morning devotionals. About the time I get the kitchen cleaned up from my breakfast, Harry is up fixing his breakfast. After another kitchen clean-up, I then have about an hour to do some laundry, clean up part of the house, or work on the paperwork piled up on the desk before I have to start preparing Harry's dinner. Theeeen, clean the kitchen again, more housework or paperwork (or both), run an errand, and, around 4:00 p.m., work outside mowing, planting, weeding, watering until dusk. I lock up the animals around 8:15 p.m., as my neighbor's lights warn me that it almost dark. A quick bite of dinner (hopefully, something I don't have to cook) and about a half-hour to unwind before showering and dropping into bed, somewhere between 10:00 - 10:30 p.m. The summer rat-race has begun!

With several checking accounts, there is always one to be balanced. That was my "between-Harry's-breakfast-and-lunch" chore this morning. Of course, it didn't balance right away. It was $29.82 off, which turned out to be two mistakes. Fortunately, I found both of them quickly and got it balanced to the penny. I fixed Harry's dinner and had it ready at 1:00 p.m., then showered and changed and ran errands from 2:00 to 4:00. I think I'm on a treadmill, but I can't figure out how to turn the darn thing off! And the doctor wants to know if I exercise?! Hmmpf! Just follow me around for a day or two, Doc!

Harry has been installing a drip watering system around the small trees in the pasture, and I am transplanting seedlings, getting ready to start outside planting **after** May 15. I've planted a few, frost-resistant things like cabbage, broccoli, peas, and some herbs, but the not-so-tolerant things like tomatoes, peppers, beans, potatoes, corn, melons, squash, etc, have to wait. Actually, that's okay, because we still have to extend the garden fencing before I can plant all those things.

May 9, 2002

We've had such beautiful weather here it has lulled me into a false sense of security. Tuesday night, we had a hard frost that wiped out my Irises, my beautiful Sun Azalea, one rose that had dared to bloom, and some of my peonies. Ohhhhhh poop! I think I hear Mother Nature sitting back chuckling "Ha, ha! Gotcha!" They say not to plant anything in this area before May 15th, and I couldn't agree more! The last couple of days there has been a cold wind blowing that feels like it's coming off an ice pack, but there isn't any snow around here, so I don't know *from whence it came.*

My seven little Araucanas stick together. Wherever one goes, the other six follow. If one goes out of the chicken coop, five others follow behind, zip, zip, zip, zip, zip, like a string of baby Quail. However, one little guy, number seven, always seems to get left behind, and he consistently winds up at the tail end of whatever they are doing, so I have named him Caboose!

I have had a little, Buff Brahma bantam sitting on a clutch of nine eggs, for over a week, and I had her locked safely in the nursery area. Today, while I was gone, Harry opened the side door and let her out into the nursery yard, which is only *partially* fenced. She got out into the main chicken yard, then

222

into the coop, but couldn't get back to her eggs. I didn't find her until 4:00 p.m. today, and I don't know how long she had been off the nest. If it was several hours (as I suspect) and the eggs got too cold, they may not hatch. Why he let her out is beyond me, but I'm thinking about putting my hands around his neck and choking him until his eyes bulge. I'm allowed to do that! It's in the Wives' Bill of Rights!

The garden planter beds are in and, today, I got the circular-garden wall blocks in place for the herb garden in the front yard. Next week, I'm going to get a load of compost and then, a load of mulch. The compost will go in the herb bed— some in the garden and some around already established plants. Then, a good heavy mulch in the flower beds to help smother out weeds. Distributing all that compost and mulch should give me about two weeks of good steady work. Somewhere in there, I should be able to start planting. In my spare time? Ha! Someone once said to me, "Don't you get bored, staying home?" I think I laughed for ten minutes before I was able to answer. When have I ever had *time* to be bored?!

I mowed the pasture again a couple of nights ago, and there is a small, white-seeded weed that is now growing out there. When you mow across it, it fogs up in a white cloud, and boy, does it cause allergies. I'm not sure exactly what the weed is, but I think it is Ventenata. By the time I'm through mowing, my eyes are watering, my nose is running, and I'm wheezing and coughing. Thank goodness for Stinging Nettle. I dump some tincture in a glass of water, and in about fifteen minutes, my breathing is back to normal. . . and no side affects!

The pasture also has an abundance of Buckthorn Plantain, Canadian Thistle, California Poppies (I wish they'd kept them in California—they are so invasive!), foxtails (ugh), Turkey Mullein, Nutsedge, Red Sorrel, Teasel, a variety of grasses, and, of course, miscellaneous blackberries. And gophers!

I sent an article, entitled *Spring is For The Birds,* to the State of Oregon Master Gardener's Quarterly Newsletter, in Dallas, Oregon. They are going to print it in their next newsletter and I'm doing another one about gophers, for their Fall newsletter. This newsletter goes out to all the Master Gardeners in the State of Oregon. Unfortunately, there is no pay involved. Now, if I could just get something published that produced a paycheck! Oh, well. Maybe someday.

It's eight o'clock and time to get the cats fed and the chickens locked up for the night. Then, I'm off for a hot soak in a bathtub full of olive oil and lavender fragrance. With any luck, maybe I'll get to bed before ten o'clock tonight, but I wouldn't count on it. Anyway, I'll wish you goodnight and hope all your dreams are good one. Love and prayers,

Shirlene and Harry

May 20, 2002

Everything is now old news, but it has taken me this long to get back to this, just to get it printed! Stop the merry-go-round! I want to get off!

May 27, 2002

Dear Friends and Family,

Congratulate me! I'm a mother! My little bantam that sat on her eggs so diligently, finally hatched out one, little, black-and-buff chick about three days ago. This morning, when I went out to feed, I discovered she had a second chick, probably hatched out yesterday. This one is buff-colored, with black on its back. They are so tiny, not much bigger than a good-sized cotton ball, and Mama is so protective of her two little babies. While she was off the nest, I took a look at the remaining eggs. It looked like one more was cracked, so she may hatch out another chick. I hope so. She certainly deserves something for her long vigil of sitting on those cold eggs.

Last week, I went to Medford to run errands. I came home about the middle of the afternoon, very tired from a day of running, and didn't think to go check the chickens until around 7:00 p.m.; I almost had a heart attack. Harry had been working up there earlier in the day and had left the outside door to the chicken coop open. Of course, all the chickens saw the open door and went out into the pasture. Then, Harry closed the door and went to work. The chickens couldn't get back into their pen and were locked out all afternoon on the hottest day we had, with no access to food or water.

When I discovered the chickens were out in the pasture, Mischief happened to be with me and took note of a gourmet meal on legs. She made a dive for one of the bantams. With a terrified squawk and sudden flight, the bantam made it out of reach with only the loss of a couple of feathers, and Mischief got whacked and yelled at, which sent her scurrying out of my reach. I opened the door to the chicken coop and with a long-handled fish net, herded the wayward feather dusters toward that area. The Aracuanas spotted the open door and raced inside to safety, but the big hens and Rooster Cogburn took another turn around the outside, with me in hot pursuit. (And you thought I didn't get any exercise!) On the next trip around, the big chickens all went inside—all except Rooster Cogburn. Darn rooster kept circling around the outside, squawking his protests, until I finally got close enough to net him.

On the coldest day we had, Harry let the bantam out, and she couldn't get back to the nest for several hours, and her eggs got cold. On the hottest day we have had, the chickens are locked out without water, in the pasture where the hawks and my cats can get to them. I told Harry, "We built that *Stalag 17* chicken coop and pen to protect the chickens from predators, but I think you are the chicken's worst predator, and I don't know how I'm going to protect them from you." (Maybe salted buckshot in the rear-end would work! *His* rear end, not the chickens'.)

When May 15th arrived, I planted a few things in the garden, and a few days later, planted some more seeds. Harry waited until the seeds were coming up to tell me he had to "dig up from the bottom of the planter bed" to install the drip water system, which means he dug up most of my seeds. Harry strikes again! On the positive side, Harry is in the process of installing a gate in the walkway between the chicken coop and garden, so we can get into the coop or pen area without going through the garden. That will be nice, since I don't want my garden gate left open. . . which has been done by someone who shall remain nameless! (The predator is on the loose again.)

Our goofy weather keeps fluctuating from "turn on the air conditioner," to "light a fire in the wood stove." Yesterday was hot, and we turned on the air conditioner. Today is overcast and cool, but I'm reluctant to start the stove again. It's supposed to be spring! Summer, almost. I made a batch of home-made ice cream today, so it has to be summer.

Our love and prayers,

Shirlene & Harry

June 16, 2002

Dear Friends and Family

We had a cool Spring, although not much rain, and then jumped into hot weather. I took advantage of the cool part of Spring to get (some) things planted, and now, the hot weather is encouraging everything to grOW. I've harvested peas out of the garden several times, and they are soooo good. Lots of flavor, like the ones I remember from my childhood, not like the cardboard food, now in the stores. Yesterday, Harry was working on the walkway gate going into the chicken area, and I was working in the garden. I picked *one* of the edible pea pods, washed it off and handed it to him. "Good?" I asked. "Ummmm," he nodded. "Consider that you've just been served dinner!" I told him. Beats the heck out of cooking!

I finally got my ten, little, day-old Guineas last Wednesday, the twelfth. They are tinier than baby chickens. I tried putting them under Mama, but she has her one little chick that she hatched a couple of weeks ago and wasn't interested in being foster mother, so she abandoned them the next morning. I was going to try to put them under Ditzy, my other hen that is setting, but she pecked at them, so I'm raising them in the nursery area, under a heat lamp.

My two hens that have "set," are both Buff Brahma Bantams, and they appear to be very good mothers. I named the first one to set "Mama." The second one "set" for about a week, and then, I noticed that she wasn't covering her eggs. "You ditzy hen," I told her, "if you don't cover the eggs, they won't hatch," and I kept trying to push them back under her, for which I got my hands soundly pecked. Since she was setting, but not covering the eggs, I named her Ditzy. After about ten days, I caught her off the nest and discovered why she wasn't keeping the eggs under her. This *little* Bantam was setting on

14 eggs! No wonder she couldn't keep them all under her! Since they haven't been all that well-covered, they may not hatch. She's been on those eggs for 26 days now and no sign of giving up. She's tenacious, if nothing else. I probably should have named her Churchill—*"Nevah, nevah, nevah give up!"*

I can't work out in the heat of the day because it makes me sick, so I work outside in the early morning, then do inside housework, laundry, paperwork on the desk, run errands, etc., until around 6:00 or 7:00 p.m. Then, I work outside in the garden until dark, which is now after 9:00 p.m. By the time I get inside, I'm too tired to cook, and during the week, Harry is at work (still working swing shift), so I don't have to, don't want to, and refuse to cook! I make up large batches of soup and put them in small freezer containers. When I come in at night, ready to drop, I shower and clean up, then have a bowl of soup for dinner. I have turkey, chicken, navy bean, and vegetable soup in the freezer, so I can rotate and not have to have the same thing every night. Being home- made, it is good, nourishing soup. (That canned stuff gags me.)

Last night, when we finally gave up and came in the house, it was 9:00 p.m. and almost dark. We were both tired and hungry, so I told Harry, "You have three choices for dinner. You can have Soup, or you can have *soup*, or you can have **soup**." He chose soup. Good choice!

The deer have started their yearly visits, so I suppose we will lose some plants. I was coming in from the pasture area one night last week and surprised four of them in the back yard. The cute little "Bambi" fawn that was here the first year we came, is now a two-prong buck, and he was heading for my Hosta plant as I came around the corner of the house. I waved my arms, and the four of them splashed up the creek, hopefully, to find someone else's yard to devastate.

Last year, the deer killed three or four of our young fruit trees, so we have surrounded the remaining ones with fencing and bird netting. A small portion of my garden is fenced, but the major portion is still open, although we have the posts and wire and Harry will soon begin to close it in. I just hope we get it done before things grow to an edible meal for our four-legged marauders. My offer still stands. If you want to go deer hunting this fall, we can set you up right here on the property.

We have new neighbors but haven't met them yet. I've been praying that we wouldn't get someone with teenagers with loud, boom boxes (is there any other kind?) It has been so peaceful back here. I would hate to see that tranquility destroyed.

And speaking of destroyed, it appears our beautiful, big trees in the back yard have succumbed to disease and may have to be taken down. Don't, as yet, know how we will go about accomplishing that, but will probably put it off until September. Too much to do this summer. It will be terribly hot here without our big trees, but they didn't leaf out this year. If they are dead, we'll need to get them down, so they won't fall on the house. Another job to put on the "to do" list.

We've had a rather windy spring, and the wind has sucked the water out of the ground like a blood-sucking leech. It seems I'm watering constantly and still can't keep up with it. We have such a large yard that, in spite of all the watering I try to do, parts of it dry up and die. If we have to take the trees out, it will be even worse. We don't have trees in the front section of the yard, so I recently planted a Ginkgo tree, but it is only about two feet tall, and they are very slow-growing trees. They live to be over a hundred years old, but it takes them half of that time to grow to be of any size. I'll be long gone before this one is of any great size. Planted for future generations!

Never mind June 21st. Without a set calendar date, I can always tell when summer has arrived. Harry says, "Uhhh . . .how much half and half does it take to make ice cream?" Now I ask you, is that a subtle hint? Our ice cream freezer sure gets a workout during the summer months. Vanilla, pineapple, sometimes strawberry—when I can get fresh ones and know where and how they are grown—and occasionally, chocolate ice cream. I've planted a bed of twenty-five Tri-star everbearing, and twenty-five Ozark Beauty everbearing strawberries. If the deer or birds don't get them before we get the fence up, we'll have fresh strawberry ice cream this year. After this year, we should have our major, garden area all fenced and not have to worry about critters. It just takes a long time to get everything accomplished.

Last night, I spotted a baby bird out of the nest, on the lawn, trying to learn to fly. We have several batches of birds that have hatched out, so I didn't know which bird house this one came from, or I would have helped it back home. I locked up two of the cats, however, C.C. wouldn't come in. She almost never does. Sure enough, I found the dead, baby bird on the lawn this morning. She didn't eat it, just killed it by playing with it. I spotted a lizard on one of the plants near the drive and warned him to go hide before the cats find him. Then, I looked closer and realized he was dead—the cats had already found him. Darn cats.

I was working in my little kitchen garden, near the back deck, and looked up at a coiled snake, a couple of feet in front of me. It was a gopher snake, and they are the 'good guys,' so I backed out of the garden and wished him well. I'm not afraid of gopher snakes, but I still wouldn't want them on me. I guess he must have taken my "Have a good day," as a personal invitation because Harry came home a couple of hours later, and said he caught a gopher snake just as he was ready to climb up the front steps. I said, "That must be Charlie, from the back garden."

Harry said, "Charlie?"

"Yeah," I told him. "If he's going to hang around here, he has to have a name. What did you do with him?"

"I took him out to the creek and turned him loose. I should have put him down a gopher hole."

Sure wish he had. If he's going to live here, he'd better start earning his keep! We haven't seen him since (for which I'm thankful), so he must have had his feelings hurt when he wasn't invited in for tea.

Harry is taking a much-deserved nap this afternoon, and it is almost time for me to go up to the garden area and start the nightly watering. When Harry gets up . . . and the temperature outside drops a bit, I'm hoping to persuade him to rototil the chicken yard. The chickens go crazy with all that fresh-turned dirt to dig in. It accomplishes several things; keeps the chicken yard clean so it keeps down disease; gives the chickens a chance to dig up and eat any bugs that might be hiding and hatching in the soil; turns the chicken fertilizer under. When I turn the chickens into my main garden area this winter, their current chicken yard will become my winter garden area. Bet I'll be able to grow almost anything in there.

Do you know what you get when you cross a Praying Mantis with a termite? You get a bug that offers thanks before he eats your house! Don't remember where I read that, but I thought it was cute. With that, I'd better end this gab session. It's time to go work outside. Remember, if you're bored, I can solve it. No time to be bored around here.

My love to all,

Shirlene and Harry

July 26, 2002

Dear Friends & Family,

I saw a bumper sticker this week that pretty well sums it up. It said, "I'm smiling because . . .I haven't got a clue about what's going on."

Well, that's about the way I feel. I get so busy I don't know which end is up! To add to the confusion, we've had several fires in the outlying areas that have increased the heat in our area, by about fifteen degrees. I'm guessing that the fires are about ten to fifteen miles, as the crow flies, so they are far enough away that they probably won't be a threat to our area, but the smoke and heat drift our way.

We get an evening wind through this area that would normally cool things off, but with the heat and the wind, it sucks the moisture out of the ground like a vampire sucking blood! I've been mulching the garden with straw, and that seems to be helping. Our well isn't able to keep up with all the watering for this acre and a third, so I have turned off the sprinklers in the back yard and am letting it die out. It breaks my heart, because it's so pretty when it is green, but there just isn't enough water. Something had to go. Our creek dried up about a week ago. This is the second year in a row. We had some rain this past winter, but not enough snow pack, so no 'year-round' creek.

Harry went across the dry, creek bed and picked black-berries yesterday, and today, I made a blackberry cobbler. I'll make a pie out of the next batch. The only good thing about the creek being dried up is that we have easy access to the berries on the other side.

Remember in my last letter, I mentioned Ditzy, the little hen that was on fourteen eggs? Well, she finally managed to hatch out one little chick. Two days later she hatched another one, so I called them Pete and Re-Pete! (Don't know if they're roosters or hens.) They are now about three weeks old. Mama, my first hen to set, has weaned her one little chick that I named Uno, and she is back on the nest again. That little nursery area is sure getting a work-out.

The Aracuanas are full grown, the Guineas are about half grown, and the garden looks like a jungle. I have one tomato plant that is at least five feet tall, equally wide, loaded with tomatoes, and is still growing. When I'm planting all those *little tiny seeds*, I somehow forget that they will grow to be **GREAT BIG PLANTS!** I always over-plant!

Harry didn't get the posts set or the fencing around the extended garden section completed, until the first week of July. I couldn't wait for him to finish or I wouldn't have had a garden again this year, so my garden was already planted and growing by the time he finished. And, he finished just in time. The week after he finished, I found deer tracks all around the outside of the garden. If it hadn't been fenced, I wouldn't have had any garden left! With the fires and everything drying up, the deer are looking for food. Harry couldn't put the fencing over the top because there were plants growing where he needed to set the center posts, so the top will have to be finished this fall, after the garden is through. Next year, it will all be completed and ready to go! Praise God!

The wasps are bad this year, so I made some wasp traps, yesterday, and put them out. I save my two-liter, Ginger Ale bottles, rinse them, cut a one-half-inch upside-down V (^) about four inches from the bottom, bend it back (on the outside) just far enough for the wasps to crawl in; put two or three inches of water in the bottom and hang a piece of smelly meat or cat food suspended just above the water. Put the cap on the bottle, leaving enough string extended outside to hang the bottle. The wasps find the opening to get inside, can't seem to find their way out again, become exhausted, fall in the water and drown. I have to empty the dead wasps and re-fill the traps every few days, but it's simple, inexpensive, effective, and no poisons! I've trapped quite a few wasps this way.

I went to the doctor Wednesday, July 24th and had a growth cut out of my eyebrow, and will go back next Wednesday, the 31st, to have the stitches removed and get the biopsy report. The doctor said, "Go home and lie down for the rest of the afternoon. If you don't, the fluid from the anesthesia will run down into your eyelid, and you could get a black eye." No problem. I figured if I get a black eye, I'll just tell everyone, "I won the fight. You should see the other guy!"

My hands are getting much worse, so if you have a prayer list, I would appreciate it if you could pray that God will help me find a good Hand Clinic, with doctors who specialize in hand surgery. I'll probably have to have one hand operated on this fall (maybe, late October—only three months away) after the garden is finished. If I don't get something done, I'm not going to be able to do a garden, or much else, by next summer.

I'll leave you with a couple of cute jokes I found.

A man walked into the library and asked the Librarian, "Can you help me find a book that I want to check out?"

"What's the name of the book?" she inquired.

"It's called *Men! The Superior Sex,*" he replied.

She answered, "It's in the second aisle on the left, under Fiction."

A minister was preparing a sermon for the next morning's services when his wife walked in and requested that he dry the dishes.

"I'm sorry," he told her, "but I'm preparing my sermon for tomorrow morning. I'm doing the Lord's work, so I won't be able to help you."

She turned and left the room, but came back a few minutes later, carrying her Bible. "Listen to this," she said, as she read from 2 Kings 21:13. "*. . . and I will wipe Jerusalem as a man wipeth a dish, wiping it and turning it upside down.*" If the Lord does dishes, you can do dishes, too."

He wiped the dishes.

With that, I will close, wishing you good health and God's peace in your life.

Our love and prayers,

Shirlene & Harry

September 20, 2002

Dear Friends and Family,

Back in the twelfth and thirteenth century, before the days of Christopher Columbus, people thought the world was flat, and if you sailed too far out to sea, you would fall off the edge of the earth. Since many ships were lost at sea and never returned, it seemed like a logical conclusion. It's been so long since I've written, you probably think I fell off the edge of the earth. Well, you're right. I did! That seems as good an explanation as any.

Summer was super busy, trying to keep up with the yard, garden, animals, housework, run errands, pay bills and take care of a mountain of paperwork that always threatens to collapse on my head. My days start at 7:00 a.m. and don't stop (outside) until around 9:30 p.m., when it is too dark to see what I am doing. By the time I come in, shower, eat, cleaned the kitchen or whatever else demands my time, I usually get in bed around 11:00. Not nearly enough sleep for me, so I am glad to see the sun setting earlier. I'm now managing to get in bed by 10:00, which is an improvement.

I can't say I'm any less busy though. Now I'm harvesting things out of the garden, and canning some of the produce. Yesterday morning I made dill pickles, and yesterday afternoon, I made Bread and Butter pickles. First time for those. Hope they turn out all right. I've also canned Chow-Chow (my first time for that) and will try to get some tomatoes canned tomorrow. We had an abundance of yellow, crook neck squash, so I made some squash puree and put it in the freezer. I purchased apples at the local farmer's market and will try to get my applesauce and apple pies made next week, and I chopped bell peppers and put them into the freezer, to use in meat loaf, fried potatoes, salads, etc. I also canned some gingered watermelon rind, to go in a fruitcake recipe that uses all dried fruit, instead of the candied fruit.

I harvested my potatoes and acorn squash and, since we don't have a cold storage, had Harry help me put down a couple of moving pallets and put straw bales around them. We didn't have enough straw, so the next day I got more bales and finished putting a second layer on top, covered the bottom with a thick layer of straw, placed the potatoes and acorn squash inside, and covered them with straw. I found a really good buy on a big bag of onions, so that also went into the straw cold storage.

I've planted my kitchen/winter garden, and I'm fighting a buck deer that is doing his best to destroy it. He's stripped a couple of tomato plants that are in the front and back yards (not in the enclosed garden area), and ate the tops off my kale plants that were coming along nicely. I think this is the "Bambi" that was here the summer we moved in. I'm relatively certain it's a buck because *does* usually travel in twos or more, and this is a single deer. From the hoof print, he's not overly large, about right for a two-year-old.

We've also had a predator that tried to dig under the gate to get into the chicken area. He stopped when he hit the wire that was buried below the gate. Wire is buried down about eighteen inches, all the way around the chicken and garden area, and after seeing what our nocturnal visitor tried, I'm surely glad I insisted on that safety feature. Harry didn't think it was necessary. I didn't recognize the track, so I'm not sure what kind of visitor, other than the fact that he likes chicken. (Probably fried, with gravy and biscuits.)

I snapped green and yellow wax beans and pickled them for winter salads. I'm hoping my corn, which got planted rather late, will mature before the weather gets cold. It looks like I've got about three dozen ears, or more, which should get us all the way through the winter. I had a volunteer cantaloupe plant that has seventeen or eighteen melons on it. They are small, and I'm not sure if they will mature before it gets cold, as with many of my tomatoes. I have tomato plants that are at least seven feet tall and an abundance of green tomatoes, but they don't seem to want to ripen. I've heard other gardeners in the area, and even a friend in Idaho, say the same thing. Large plants, prolific production, but not ripening very well. My okra didn't produce as well as I had hoped, and I still have celery to harvest. Ask me what I'm doing in my "spare" time!

Actually, what I'm doing in my spare time is taking a computer class, and I hope to find time (soon) to go to the library and search the Internet for hand clinics on the West Coast. Yes, I'm still having problems with my hands, and they are getting worse every day. I'm trying to wait until all the gardening, harvesting and processing is done, but it looks like I may ultimately have to have surgery, so please keep that in prayer. I can no longer put my right hand down flat on the table because the thumb is curved under, into the palm, and I can no longer use the right thumb on the space bar when I type. Too painful! I'm trying to learn to use my left thumb on the space bar, which slows me down to a snail's pace and makes me feel as though I have my hands on backwards. When I tell my left thumb to hit the space bar, my brain keeps saying, "does not compute . . . does not compute!" Soooo, another reason you haven't heard from me—typing is becoming a bit of a challenge, and holding a pen to write is becoming impossible. I'm now having the store clerks make out the check, and then I sign it.

We've had such hot weather this summer because of the surrounding fires, so it was a real surprise when the nights suddenly dropped down to 40 degrees. I decided I'd better get my house plants inside before we get any frost, but before I move them inside each fall, I like to clean my carpets. Oh, goodie! Another project! I managed to get the living room, dining room, kitchen, hallway, both bathrooms and the den shampooed, but I still have to do the sewing/storage room, and the two bedrooms. I know what you're thinking . . . if I didn't goof off so much, I probably could have had it finished.

My grandkids visited the 13th and 14th of this month and got to help plant peas for my winter garden and help with some of the harvesting, and Parker weeded the garden and fed the weeds to the chickens and Guineas. They got to name the last two chicks that were hatched. Brantley named one chick

Lady, "Because she stands up straight and tall," and Parker named the other chick Carrot. No explanation on that one. Draw your own conclusions. I don't know who enjoyed the time more, me or the kids, but I certainly wish they lived close enough to add their little hands to my routine.

Last year, I invested in a new bed, an Englander with a pillow top, and it has been a real blessing, but recently, I discovered a coil coming through the side. I called the retailer, he contacted Englander, and they took my mattress to Portland to fix it. They left me a 'loaner' mattress and, after a couple of nights on it, I called the retailer. "I know this mattress you left me must be made of your very best, top quality . . . cement," I told him. I don't think that is what he expected me to say. Anyway, after two-and-a-half weeks, they are bringing my mattress back tomorrow. Hallelujah!

Saturday is farmer's market day, so I'd better close and get in bed, or I'll never be able to get up in the morning. I leave you with the following thought-for-the-day.

A little boy heard the minister say "From dust ye came, to dust ye shall return." Later, at home, he looked at all the dust bunnies under his bed and declared, "Somebody's either coming or going under my bed!"

My love and prayers,

Shirlene and Harry

September 24, 2002

D ear Friends and Family,

When I finished feeding, watering and locking up the animals for the night, there were about thirty minutes of daylight left, so I sat in the porch swing on the back deck and watched the sun play hide and seek with the mountain, eventually hiding on the other side. There is a special quiet about this time of evening that I love. The daytime animals have stopped hunting and feeding and have sought shelter for the night, and the night hunters have not yet started to prowl. The sun has disappeared from sight, but the darkness has not yet descended. The earth takes a long, deep breath and holds it, pausing in its frantic rush. I, too, pause from my frantic pace and enjoy the quiet beauty that surrounds me. Even the wind has ceased from its earlier rushing to and fro. A cool, whisper-soft breath of air, not even enough to move the leaves, caresses my cheek like a gentle lover, promising cooler nights and days, soon.

I don't need a watch to tell me when it is time to go inside. Crickets in the dry creek sing the descending darkness into being, and a couple of frogs, who must have found a mud puddle to survive the drought, add their harmony to the melody. Two years ago when the creek flowed all summer, it was so full of frogs they sounded like the Anvil Chorus. There are few left this summer, so their music is softer, but all the more sweet for the rarity of it.

Leaves are starting to fall off the trees now, and when the wind blows, they skim across the dry lawn like tiny sailboats being blown across a lake. The summer garden is still producing, but winding down, some of it already turned brown, and the winter garden is beginning to grow, but not yet producing. A nice time to pause, before winter sets in.

I defrost my freezer twice a year, in March and September, so today I tackled my less-than-favorite chore. I removed everything, put it in the freshly scrubbed laundry tub and poured ice over it, turned the freezer off, propped the door open, and went about my business. Big mistake! I got busy with a couple of other tasks and forgot about the freezer, which sat there quietly defrosting. My first clue that I had a problem was when I stepped into the laundry room, and the carpet went "squish!" The song, *Row, Row, Row Your Boat,* immediately came to mind. Thank goodness I have a good carpet cleaner. I spent the next hour vacuuming water out of the carpet and getting it dried out. The pathetic thing is that I'll probably do the same dumb thing again next March! I *used to be* a multi-tasked person, one who could have several different things going at the same time and keep everything up in the air, like a juggler. Surprise, surprise! Not any more! I've now got a one-track mind, and most of the time, *that* track is de-railed! Now, everything is organized chaos, and I have to look on my driver's license to remember my name.

I had to remove my little Buff Brahma Bantams out of the main chicken pen, into the nursery area, because the Guineas were ganging up on them, trapping them in a corner, trying to peck them to death. My neighbor says Guineas can be somewhat carnivorous, so I guess they figured those little Bantams were mealtime. Ol' Rooster Cogburn is still the only stud in the hen house, but being a bantam, and being ganged up on by the Guineas, he's now locked in the nursery area with the other bantams and can't get to his harem. This has greatly reduced his paternal services, and he's not very happy about it. The hens are getting a rest, so they don't seem to mind. The other day I saw one of the large hens parading by on the other side of the fence, with her tongue stuck out at him, saying, "Nanner, nanner, nanner."

October 8, 2002

October first dawned sunny, but with a cool nip in the air. We get our newspaper delivered around 5:00 or 5:30 p.m., and I rarely walk down the lane to get it, so Harry brings it in with him at 2:00 a.m. By the time I read Tuesday's paper, it is Wednesday morning, and the weather report is already past tense. I haven't had the TV on, so I also missed the weather report on television.

Last year we didn't have a hard frost until sometime in November, but I had an eerie feeling it was going to freeze the first of October. It did! The only thing I can figure out is that God must have had the Gardening Angel sitting on my shoulder, because I decided I'd better go ahead and harvest whatever I wanted out of the garden—ripe or not. The next morning, the entire garden was mush! The freeze put an end to this year's garden as effectively as a curtain dropping on a stage at the end of Act III.

The ones who benefited from it were my chickens and Guineas. I closed off the main chicken yard and opened the nursery yard gate, so the Bantams could have that area, and I opened the gate to one section of the garden for the Guineas and big chickens. They thought they'd died and gone to Heaven! Any leaf that did not instantly freeze was immediately plucked by a greedy chicken or Guinea, and any weed trying to grow was instantly gobbled up. They're doing an excellent job of scratching and fertilizing the soil in my planter beds, and digging up any bugs trying to hide in the soil. Later this winter, after the garden extension area is fenced across the top, I'll turn them into that area. By spring, my garden should be well-plowed and ready to plant, thanks to my "chicken tractors."

Two years of drought and a summer of rampaging fires have been extremely hard on the wild animals. As their food supplies dwindle, they become desperate and increasingly bolder. All summer, the deer have circled my enclosed garden area, trying to get in, eating anything that grows through the wire fencing. Some small predator, probably a skunk, has repeatedly tried to dig under the gate to the chicken pen, and at various points around the perimeter, fortunately, to be stopped by the buried wire extending eighteen inches into the ground.

After my freezer defrosting fiasco, I decided I'd better get out the carpet cleaner and finish the bedrooms, back sewing/storage room, and the laundry room. So, on the 26th of September, I started moving things out of the way to shampoo my remaining carpets. The sewing/storage room backs up to the deck, so when I got to that area, I moved things onto the back deck until the carpet dried. When I moved articles back inside, I decided to leave my basket of apples on the porch, as the nights were getting cooler, and I felt the apples would keep well out there. I kept them there last winter with no problems.

I went to bed around 10:00 p.m., tired but satisfied with a good day's work. Around 10:45, I heard a crash, thud, on the back deck. Since my bedroom wall backs up to the deck, and the head of my bed is against that wall, I am aware of anything that happens on the deck. My first thought was, *I'll bet those racoons are back!* I grabbed the shotgun, not sure what I might encounter, and crept quietly to the back door of the storage room. Fortunately, I'm not a stupid person, so I didn't open the door; I turned on the back light and looked out the window. A lawn chair was in front of the window and several chair cushions were stacked on top of it. All I could see was the top of a black back, above the cushions. *It couldn't be!* Nawww! Must be a stray dog!

"Lord, that has to be the biggest dog I've ever seen."

About that time, the animal raised its head and I drew in a deep breath. "Uuuuuh! **Not** a dog!" I was standing about three feet away from a good-sized black bear who was happily munching on my apples. I was thankful for the window that separated us!

I realized the shotgun wouldn't be of much help, so I put it away, waited a few minutes and went back to check on my uninvited dinner guest. He was still dining. Not wanting to leave him to take up permanent residence on my back porch, I called the Oregon State Police, Animal Control Division. They came out in about fifteen minutes. By that time, the bear was off the porch, but he had gone into the vacant, weed-overgrown lot next door. They heard him crashing around in the brush and chased him up the dry creek bed, but never got anywhere close to him. I moved my apples back inside and haven't had (to my knowledge) any more nightly visits from "Black Bart."

One thing about this household, if things get dull, just stick around for a little while and something off-the-wall will happen! The only thing I promised Harry when we got married was that life with me would never be boring. He says he hasn't been bored!

Harry is working on painting the last section of the fence and when that is done, we plan on taking a couple of days and going to the Coast, just to get out of here and take a break. As long as we're here, we're both working, so we have to get away once in a while. Even though the garden is through, there is much to do to get things ready for winter, and I've been canning as much of the produce as possible. I decided to make catsup out of some of my ripe tomatoes, so I've been working on that for the past two days. I've never made catsup before, and I can't say I'm overly thrilled by the recipe I found in one of my books. It had way too much vinegar, so I tried adding extra corn syrup and brown sugar to compensate. It doesn't taste *bad*, but it tastes . . . different. Neither Harry nor I can figure out what tastes so different, or what needs to be corrected. I'll try a different recipe next year.

I've been getting bids on lumber and materials to start building the Guinea house. I will probably go get the beginning materials tomorrow, although Harry probably won't start building until after our trip to the coast. Hope we have nice weather. Summer at the Coast can sometimes be cold as a witch's patutie, but September, October and sometimes November can have some really pleasant, balmy days. Unpredictable though, so we're hoping for good weather.

I bought Jonagold apples at the Farmer's Market and made (some of) my applesauce, but I haven't had time to make apple pies. This past weekend, some friends of mine gave me *two boxes* of Golden Delicious apples, so now I have to make more applesauce, and freeze more apples for pies. I suppose I could be generous and put some of them out for my nocturnal guest, but I really don't want to encourage him to hang around here.

After the garden froze, Harry commented, "That watermelon over by the fence is turning yellow."

"That's because it's a pumpkin," I told him.

"Oh."

The buzzer on the dryer just went off, the timer to remind me to change the water is ringing (no wonder I'm dingy!) and the chickens and Guineas are squawking for their afternoon feeding, so I guess I'd better quit this gab session and get back to work. They say there's no rest for the wicked, and since I'm not getting any rest, I guess I must be pretty wicked! 'Till next time, my love and prayers,

Shirlene and Harry

November 25, 2002

Dear Friends and Family,

On the seventh of this month, we had several days of soaking rain, saturating the ground. Then the rain stopped, and we had silver-white skies too stingy to rain, and drizzling drops of soggy fog, otherwise known as 'Oregon Mist.' Our gloomy fog is thrown across the tree tops like a shawl across a woman's shoulders. Fortunately, it is a high fog, so visibility at ground level is good, but it effectively blocks out the sun. Today, we had that bright, shiny stuff for a short while. If memory serves me correctly, I believe it's called sunshine.

This month has rushed by like a run-a-way locomotive. I spent two weeks with a good case of bronchitis and sinusitis, too sick to care if the boat sank or sailed. I finally got some antibiotics and got over my case of creepin' crude, but I lost two weeks of whatever it was I had to do, and now I'm 'behinder' than ever. (How about that new word? - behinder! Oooooo-kay!) Bet the spell check is going to have fun with that one!

I sit in my chair with my laptop on a wedge pillow, to do my typing. The other night, I happened to glance up and a rather large spider was on the upper right corner of the pillow. Sure didn't take me very long to get out of this chair and get that spider killed. I move pretty fast, for an old broad! Now I empathize with Little Miss Muffet . . . only I didn't have any curds and whey. Do you know the spell check doesn't have the word "Muffet" in it? What's wrong with those people who designed this computer program? Didn't they ever hear of Mother Goose? Didn't their parents ever read them Nursery Rhymes? That's got to be un-American!

Harry called Thursday and said he had to leave at 3:00 a.m. Friday morning to go to British Columbia, and would be home Sunday night. Well, he did leave Friday morning, but he came home Saturday night, so I figure he owes me an extra day of vacation. When he told me he would be home four days, Thanksgiving through Sunday, I told him, "What a coincidence. I'll be out of town those four days. You can hold down the fort." Wishful thinking. He just grinned. Actually, my neighbor is the one going away, and I have to be here to take care of her dogs. Hopefully, she will be able to take care of my animals at Christmas time, but I haven't asked her, yet. She was gone last year at Christmas, and I took care of the animals. This year is my turn. It's a nice trade-off.

'Tis the beginning of baking and hiding season—baking Christmas goodies, and hiding them from Harry, so I'll still have something to give out when Christmas gets here. I made two batches of fudge, no-bake oatmeal cookies, Rice Krispie treats and date pin-wheel cookies. I peeled and processed the persimmon pulp to make persimmon-oatmeal cookies (maybe tomorrow) and got out my recipe for old-fashioned ginger snaps. Will probably also make chocolate chip cookies. Much to be done between now and Christmas, but at least I have my Christmas shopping done. I start in July, and each year do less than the year before. I like decorating the house, visiting with friends, baking and sharing, but each year I get more disenchanted with the commercialism of Christmas, and concentrate more on the Savior's birth. He *is* the reason for the season. Somehow, we seem to forget.

The guinea house is framed—walls, roof, floor, windows, doors—but the inside has to be finished, so Harry is working on that, a little each day. He is building a food-storage area in one corner and enclosing it so the guineas can't roost on top of the food barrels. A nursery area will be framed in another corner, then the roosts have to be built, and an outside yard fenced in. I can't wait until it is finished, and I can separate those darn guineas from my chickens.

When I separated the bantams from the guineas, I left the Araucana hens and the three white hens, in with the

247

guineas, figuring they were bigger chickens and would probably be all right. Well, the guineas are really aggressive birds, and they rule the chicken yard. One-on-one wouldn't be bad, but they operate in gangs. (I think they have their own Mafia!) The Araucanas seem to be faring okay, but the bullies chase the Brahmas constantly, plucking out feathers. Since the Brahmas are running *away* from the guineas, the main area of attack is the rear end. I now have three Light Brahma hens with nude rear ends hanging out in the breeze. Now that the weather is dropping down into the 20's at night, those poor little hens are going to freeze their rear ends off. Literally!

November 30, 2002

Last day of November and I still haven't managed to get this letter in the mail. Like the old poem says, my get-up-and-go just got-up-and-went. I thought the winter season was supposed to be a time of rest, but if it is, that doesn't apply here. Flower beds that should have been cleaned up in early November still have dead blossoms staring back at me, accusing me of neglect. Fruit trees have to be sprayed, leaves and straw put down for mulch, debris gathered and burned, and bulbs still to be dug up, divided and replanted. (The trees and debris are Harry's job.)Two weeks of being sick this month sure threw my schedule out of whack.

God's word says, *"And we know that all things work together for good for them that love God, to them who are called according to His purpose (Romans 8:28.)* Even my two weeks of creepin' crud had a good side. When I got sick, I got out a stack of my herbal books and started looking for remedies. Unfortunately, I thought I just had a cold, so I didn't get the right remedy for bronchitis. However, in my search, I found a ginger tea that I thought would help my cold. It didn't help the bronchitis I didn't know I had, but, wonder of wonders, it helped my arthritic hands! What a blessing. The constant pain let up, and I am able to use my hands more than before. Arthritis is an inflammation of the joints, and ginger is anti-inflammatory, so it makes sense that it would help. I'm still drinking about three cups a day of the tea, and will continue to do so. If any of you have arthritis, I'm sending the recipe:

1 quart of water; 2-3 slices of lemon; 5 thin slices of ginger root; 12 whole cloves; two, 2 ½-to-3 inch cinnamon sticks. Place in pan and boil 3-5 minutes. Turn off and let steep. Strain off all spices and keep liquid in refrigerator. Makes four cups. For best results, drink 3 cups per day.

Since I drink three - four cups a day, I double the above recipe. Then, I only have to make it every other day. It only takes me about five minutes to get everything prepared and on the stove. After I heat this in the microwave, I put a teaspoon of honey in it before I drink it. It's a really good tasting tea, and it has done wonders for my arthritis. God is good!

Another thing that is *very* good for arthritis is unsul-fured, Blackstrap molasses. Two tablespoons per day.

Best I get this letter printed, folded and stuffed into en-velopes, or it will wind up being my Christmas letter. Hopefully, I will be better organized in December. (Don't laugh! It *could* happen.)

I can't remember where I read the following, but I thought it was too good not to pass on.

Here's What I Have Discovered:

God grant me the Senility to forget the people I never liked anyway, the good fortune to run into the ones I do, and the eyesight to tell the difference.

I started out with nothing and still have most of it.

My wild oats have turned into prunes and All Bran.

I finally got my head together; Now my body is falling apart.

Funny, I don't remember being absent minded.

If all is not lost, where is it?

All reports are in. Life is definitely unfair.

It is easier to get older than it is to get wiser.

Some days you're the dog; some days you're the hydrant.

I wish the buck stopped here. I sure could use a few . . .

Kids in the backseat cause accidents. Accidents in the back seat cause kids.

It's hard to make a comeback when you haven't been anywhere.

The only time the world beats a path to your door is when you're in the bathroom.

If God wanted me to touch my toes, He'd have put them on my knees.

When I'm finally holding all the cards, why does everyone decide to play chess?

Our love and prayers,

Shirlene and Harry

December 3, 2002

D ear Friends and Family,

      The house is decorated, a cozy fire in the wood stove, and Christmas Carols on the stereo. What better time to start my Christmas letter. I do my Christmas shopping from July through October and have it completed before Halloween, or may buy something "last minute" before Thanksgiving, but from Thanksgiving on, I refuse to get caught up in the Christmas shopping insanity. The nicest part about getting the shopping done ahead of time is that it leaves me with only the joy of the season—decorating the house, listening to Christmas carols and concentrating on the reason for the season—Jesus Christ. "For unto you *this day* is born in the City of David, a savior, Christ the Lord." Over two thousand years ago God sent his son to be born—a savior for all who would receive Him. He is born anew each time someone accepts him as Savior. The message never gets old.

      For all the joy of the season, many people are out of work, so there is also much stress and sadness. We try to share with those less fortunate, all year long, but even more so at this time of year. There but for the grace of God, go I! It is certainly a time to count our blessings. A warm, cozy house, an abundance of food, enough money to cover the monthly expenses, and reasonably good health, considering our age and the problems that go with it. I can always look around and see someone worse off, so there is much reason to be thankful. Harry has a week off, from Christmas through New Year's and we plan to go to Sacramento for a couple of days, weather and health permitting. If the weather is really stormy or the roads are too icy, we won't chance it.

      Our house is too small for a Christmas tree, and I really miss the smell of the pine needles. I put up the lighted Nativity, set up the lighted village, have a huge poinsettia, Advent candles, Santa Clauses scattered about, and a three-foot, decorated half-tree hanging on the wall, but I still miss the smell of a real tree. When I went to have my eyes examined Monday morning, I sat in a chair next to their seven-foot Christmas tree, and took deep breaths of the fresh pine. They probably thought I was hyperventilating.

It hasn't been much above 40 degrees for the past week, and our stove has been getting a real workout, but it has kept the house warm and comfortable. Even though I'm not Christmas shopping, I have been out running errands, so I've been caught up in the traffic and lines at the stores. I guess there's no way to avoid it during the month of December.

I took the truck to get new tires for the front, to have studded tires put on the back, and to get an alignment. They got the tires on, but forgot to do the alignment, so I had to go back the next day to have that done. I felt sorry for the people at the tire store. They were so swamped with work, the place was like a zoo. No wonder they forgot the alignment. I certainly wouldn't want their job at this time of the year.

December 11, 2002

It has been raining off and on all week, and it looks like it will continue through the weekend. We need the rain, so I'm not complaining, but it sure has made the chicken/guinea area a muddy quagmire, slick as a greased pig. I walk very carefully up there, for if I fell, it would be difficult to get up out of that slippery mess. I'd probably just slide into a corner and stay there until spring.

A few days ago, the guineas got into the bantam area, and Harry separated them and got the guineas back in their own area. Unfortunately, in the process, Rooster Cogburn got into the big chicken-guinea area. I don't know how long he was there, but when I went up in the evening to lock up, after all the birds were inside, I spotted a lump of feathers in a corner, not moving, and the head and feet not visible. "Oh, no. Those darn guineas have killed my rooster." I was sick. I went over to pick him up, to bury him. When I lifted him, he pulled his head up from under his wing and looked around. "Rooster Cogburn! You're alive!" He looked a little dazed, but he "Braaak, baak, baaked," at me while I was carrying him to his area. I think he was trying to tell me about his ordeal, and probably being thankful he was rescued. No telling how long he'd been curled up in that corner, playing dead, but it probably saved his life. Pretty smart rooster! Those darn guineas are getting entirely too aggressive. Need to get them separated, soon.

I finished some Christmas baking this morning so I could get a couple of packages ready to mail. Tomorrow, I'll stand in line to get them on their way, and hopefully, get this letter on its way to wish each and every one a

Very Merry Christmas and a
Happy (and safe) New Year.
Praising God for the blessing of
His Son,
Shirlene & Harry

P.S.   Please keep in touch. I'll write again, after the New Year.

GLOSSARY

Fibromyalgia: A form of muscular rheumatism. *Fibro=* fiber; *my=* muscle; *algia=* pain. Pain in the muscles, ligaments and tendons in the nonskeletal part of the musculoskeletal system. It affects all movement.

The American College of Rheumatology designates that if you hurt in eleven of the eighteen established tender points, you have Fibromyalgia (FM). People with FM also have an elevated sed rate, which can be determined by blood tests.

People with FM have trouble sleeping and wake up feeling as though a truck has run over them. They hurt in every part of their body, as though with a severe case of the flu, only worse.

Doctors tell patients that there is no cure, and once you have FM, you will have it all your life. There is nothing you can do other than be on medications for the rest of your life. I disagree.

It took me several years to do it, but I have managed to get rid of, or at least obtain dormancy, of my FM. It is a long road, certainly not obtainable overnight, but it can be done.

Polyneuralgia Rheumatica: Inflammation of many nerves and veins.

Although doctors give the same negative, lifetime diagnosis, no cure, and medications, I have found that (in my case) this too, was controlled, without medications!

Arrhythmia: Erratic, sometimes very rapid heartbeat. Can lead to sudden death. I have also managed to control this, naturally.

None of the above information is intended as medical advice. I am simply relating what I have managed to do about the above diagnosed illnesses. Good health is obtainable.